KITCHEN WITCHCRAFT FOR BEGINNERS

KITCHEN WITCHCRAFT
FOR
BEGINNERS

SPELLS, RECIPES, AND RITUALS TO BRING
YOUR PRACTICE INTO THE KITCHEN

DAWN AURORA HUNT

ILLUSTRATIONS BY HANNAH DAVIES

ROCKRIDGE
PRESS

Copyright © 2022 by Rockridge Press

First Rockridge Press trade paperback edition 2022

Rockridge Press and the Rockridge Press logo are trademarks or registered trademarks of Callisto Media Inc. and/or its affiliates in the United States and other countries and may not be used without written permission.

For general information on our other products and services, please contact our Customer Care Department within the United States at (866) 744-2665, or outside the United States at (510) 253-0500.

Hardcover ISBN: 979-8-88650-426-2
Paperback ISBN: 978-1-68539-512-4
eBook ISBN: 978-1-68539-732-6

Manufactured in the United States of America

Interior and Cover Designer: Tricia Jang
Art Producer: Maya Melenchuk
Editor: Alexis Sattler
Production Editor: Ellina Litmanovich
Production Manager: Holly Haydash

Illustration © 2022 Hannah Davies

10 9 8 7 6 5 4 3 2 1 0

TO GRACE,
FOR HER UNKNOWING LESSONS
OF KITCHEN MAGICK, RITUAL COOKING,
AND THE BEST MEATBALLS AND
GRAVY RECIPE ON EARTH.
"THERE'S ALL GOOD INGREDIENTS IN HERE."
THANK YOU, GRANDMA.

CONTENTS

INTRODUCTION

Welcome to my kitchen. It smells of cinnamon and vanilla, filling the senses with comfort as dried herbs hang around windows lined with crystals and jars filled with spices. Come in and sit for a spell.

My name is Dawn, and I've been a practicing kitchen witch for over two decades—more, if you count the time before I knew what a kitchen witch was. I was raised in a traditional Italian family, where food and its preparation were an almost religious experience. Many of the recipes and traditions in this book are shaped by my connection to those European traditions. However, kitchen witchcraft can be found all over the world, and learning about different practices can enrich your own. For me, I have been learning and practicing kitchen witchcraft in some way my whole life. At the age of twenty, I nonchalantly pulled a book on kitchen witchcraft off the shelf of a local bookstore. Reading the first page, I thought, "This is *me*. I am a kitchen witch!" Since then, I've read everything I could get my hands on about the practice and principles of kitchen witchcraft, food magick, and cooking with intention. My own practices, rituals, and recipes are born out of necessity, learned skills, meditation, and visualization to create magick in simple ways in the kitchen every day.

This book, and kitchen witchcraft, is not just for those who identify as witches or pagans. It is for anyone who wants to learn to be more mindful about how to channel their energy when it comes to cooking, eating, and sharing food. Whether you are a gourmet cook or a microwave maven, kitchen witchcraft is for you. If you have ever made a meal for someone you love or stirred some soup on the stove when you were feeling sick, then you, dear reader, unknowingly sprinkled a little intention and magick into that food.

HOW TO USE THIS BOOK

In these pages, you'll discover many tools, practices, and mindset shifts to create a sacred space in the kitchen for magickal workings every day. Part 1 of this book features the basic how-tos and to-dos of kitchen witchcraft. It will help inspire you to grow your own individual practice by learning what ingredients and utensils to keep on hand and how to build a kitchen altar to focus energies and welcome spiritual entities.

By exploring basic spells and easy recipes in part 2, you can incorporate magick into your everyday life that can be worked in the kitchen as well as in other parts of the home. Once you're done with the basics, you'll explore the Wheel of the Year and see how to celebrate the turning of the seasons with your newfound kitchen witch skills. Once you've got your heart, mind, and kitchen set up for this kind of spiritual work, you can easily use this book as a guide for easy recipes and inspiration to build your practice. So, settle in at your kitchen table, nibble on something delicious, and get ready to stir up some magick on your journey into kitchen witchcraft.

PART I

CREATING A WITCH'S SACRED SPACE IN THE KITCHEN

Welcome to your first step into kitchen witchcraft! Part 1 of this book is going to give you some basic background on witchcraft and the lore surrounding it. You are going to explore what it means to practice kitchen witchcraft and how it is different from and similar to other forms of magickal arts. You might be surprised at how easy it is to get in touch with your inner witch and how many of these practices you have already been doing daily without realizing it. This section will show you how simple it can be to see your kitchen as a sacred space and set up a magickal altar of any shape or size that suits your needs and values. By the time you've gotten through this section, your pantry will be stocked with the right ingredients, your modern cauldrons will be bubbling away happily, and you will have your trusty wooden spoon ready to whip up delicious meals brimming with magickal intention.

CHAPTER 1
DISCOVERING THE WITCH WITHIN

How would one find the *witch within*, or more important for this book, how would one find the *kitchen witch within*? Witches are people who use metaphysical practices, rituals, spells, and intention to effect change or channel energy. They can be individuals who commune with nature, follow the rhythms of the seasons, help and heal whenever possible, and believe in the power of magick. Within the next few pages, you'll learn basic principles and practices of witchcraft. Whether you already identify as a witch or are just learning what kind of witchcraft interests you, these next few chapters will lend you some guidance on how, and where, to start. As this book begins, so does your journey into finding your inner witch, turning your magickal spark into a comforting flame to light your way along this path.

WHAT DOES IT MEAN TO BE A WITCH?

People who identify as witches do not all practice the same thing. They walk a multitude of spiritual paths, and their practices vary as much as their fingerprints. Modern witches might practice rituals, cast spells, meditate, work with crystals, chart astrology, read tarot cards, do yoga, use manifestation for spiritual goals, or worship particular gods or goddesses. They often find commonality in things like valuing a connection to nature, deities, or spirits; honoring the turning of the Wheel of the Year; or celebrating the solstices and equinoxes.

Witchcraft, like many spiritual practices, may be part of family traditions handed down for generations. Some people may be taught these ideals and rituals by family elders, but it is also common for witches today to find, cultivate, and grow their own individual practices. They may learn from their own research, friends, or communities, and might practice alone or in groups. Either or both may be right for you. You may be drawn to large community rituals yet enjoy a solitary everyday practice. Your practice is your practice–embrace it.

MAGICK IS MORE THAN SPELLS & POTIONS

Magick isn't just spells and potions. It is a deep trust in your own power and will to effect change, harness energy, and create outcomes by working with universal energies. You can participate in a public ritual or perform a spell without necessarily identifying as a witch. Finding the path of witchcraft and walking it long enough to know being a witch is who you are, not just what you do, is the journey of magick.

Most witches, even those who have similar beliefs or devotions, practice slightly differently. They pull from many different practices to create something wholly their own. Often it is this free-flowing construct that attracts people to the path in the first place. A common thread in most witchcraft and neo-pagan practice is a deep reverence for the earth and nature and following the old Pagan calendar, also called the Wheel of the

Year. Some witches might commune with the spirit realm psychically, some might worship gods from many pantheons, some might practice the arts of healing. Most pull from any practice that makes them feel closer to their spiritual selves. Throughout all traditions and practices, one thing witches have in common is harnessing energy and intention to affect their world and achieve spiritual and personal goals.

A NOTE ON CLOSED PRACTICES & APPROPRIATION

Witches can build personal practices by mingling traditions and magick from many different backgrounds, so it is especially important to educate yourself and build your practice carefully and respectfully. Because of the wide swath of spiritual practices in the world, it is possible to unintentionally appropriate a closed practice. There are many traditions that have been handed down for years within communities, and some are open, some are closed. An open tradition means that it is considered open to a wider audience by the community that developed it. A closed practice means that this is something that should not be participated in unless you are a member of that community, initiated into the tradition by the community.

The difference between an open and closed practice may not be evident, so doing proper research through reading and studying reliable sources is crucial. Being called to a practice that might not be rooted in your cultural upbringing means learning and educating yourself on where those traditions came from, how they are used, and why. In witchcraft, intentionality and specificity matter. If a practice is closed, permission to practice must granted by said community.

THE MANY WAYS TO PRACTICE WITCHCRAFT

There are numerous practices like Cottage Witchcraft, Green Witchcraft, and Garden Witchcraft that can all be incorporated or intermingled with kitchen witchcraft. For example, a cottage witch has a practice that centers around home and nurturing those they consider family. A garden witch's sacred space is the garden or yard, and they are most connected to their spiritual self when working with all plants. Green witchcraft is a well-known practice that incorporates more of the natural world, focusing on things like foraging for mushrooms and, in some cases, animal husbandry and farming. All these practices are akin to kitchen witchcraft, centering around home, family, and nurturing. They are just some of the home-based practices that can be used by self-taught solitary practitioners or those who seek more formal instruction. These practices and magick can be mixed and matched to create whatever works for you.

WHY KITCHEN WITCHCRAFT IS A GREAT PLACE TO START

If you are just starting your journey, the kitchen is a wonderful place to begin. Kitchen witchcraft is foundational for many types of magick. It's a hands-on, simple-ingredients, everyday kind of practice. It is perfect for people who have no previous knowledge of witchcraft at all or for seasoned witches looking to weave their current practice more deeply into their everyday life. You may already incorporate intentions into your cooking, whether you realize it or not. Kitchen witchcraft provides the practitioner with perspective and connection, not just to the magick you are doing but to the natural world around you, to the season, to the plants and animals who give their lives for food to eat, and to those who gather around the table.

STRENGTHENING YOUR CONNECTION TO NOURISHING INGREDIENTS

Applying mindfulness to food can reconnect you to the ingredients, thereby deepening your connection to the earth. If you live in a place that has four seasons, you might think twice about eating watermelon in January even if you are craving it. In this case, the length of time an ingredient has been in transit and the geography of where it came from come into question. Even if you live where the climate does not change all year, there are still foods that are native to your region. Being able to identify whether a food is something the earth is providing at the time of choosing can also increase mindfulness and may deepen your connection to the ingredients you are using for nourishment and magick, bonding you to Mother Earth energy and life source vibration. This is a key component of kitchen witchcraft.

CREATING THE SACRED EVERY DAY

Kitchen witchcraft is an amazingly straightforward way to create the sacred every day because of the familiar tasks and tactile nature of the practice. When performing daily kitchen tasks, having knowledge of the energetic properties of food can flip the proverbial switch to help you see the magick in the process. For example, if you were craving a cup of spiced chai, your own knowledge of the ingredients in chai (cinnamon, cloves, and ginger, for example) could tell you that these are all spices associated with prosperity. By being mindful of the ingredients, and by pouring and sipping the tea with intention and visualization aligned with prosperity, you have just performed kitchen witchcraft. Once you are mindful of the energetic properties of common household ingredients, you will learn how to incorporate magickal workings in convenient ways throughout the day.

HOW TO EMBRACE YOUR INNER WITCH

In recent years, depictions of witchcraft have had a renaissance in movies, TV shows, and social media. The increased interest in the occult and all things witchy is great, but it also allows for the spread of misinformation or stereotyping. Finding credible sources, listening to your own spiritual intuition, and studying practices that excite you are all parts of finding the witch within. The real work of embracing your inner witch comes from knowing yourself, believing in the power of your will, and learning to harness the power of intention. It is a working journey of self-discovery, in and through witchcraft.

You have picked up this book on kitchen witchcraft, which suggests you already hear a hollering in your heart of a magickal path. Embracing your inner witch is a lifelong process of learning, growing, outgrowing, and learning again. To truly become a witch and practitioner of magick, you must first start with an open mind and heart to your chosen path. This means that your path is your own. As you embrace your inner witch, you may change direction, taking what works and leaving what does not serve you. All of it is uniquely perfect for you, wherever your path of witchcraft may lead.

CONCLUSION

Now that you have taken your first steps to discovering your own inner witch, it's time to cross the threshold into the kitchen. By learning how and what witches practice far beyond potions and spells, you have seen how your craft can be whatever you make it. Through the many ways to practice and study the craft, finding your own path can be a rewarding and lifelong journey. As you will learn in this book, so much simple magick starts in the kitchen, and it may be already happening on a subconscious level. With a little bit of knowledge, you'll be able to hone this energy to begin or enrich your spiritual, energetic, and magickal practices. As with a fantastic recipe, you add a pinch of this and a dash of that to create something unique and satisfying.

≫ KEY TAKEAWAYS:

✦ Being a witch is not just about what you do. It's about finding your own path that is uniquely you.

✦ Be especially aware of closed practices and cultural traditions. Do your research and always be respectful and willing to learn so that you do not unintentionally appropriate or offend others.

✦ While there are many hearth and home witchcraft practices, kitchen witchcraft is the one that focuses most on food, recipes, and cooking.

✦ Mindfulness can help you strengthen your connection to the earth and your ingredients.

CHAPTER 2

THE ORIGINS OF KITCHEN WITCHCRAFT

Now that you have explored what it can mean to walk the path of witchcraft, it's time to enter the heart of the home: the kitchen. In this chapter, you will learn concepts you can use to center your magickal practice around home and family. You will learn about the history, folklore, and origins of kitchen witchcraft as it was practiced long before it was named as such. This chapter will also guide you into deeper knowledge of the tenets and values that have influenced the development of this form of witchcraft for centuries, helping it stand the test of time. Though each kitchen witch's rituals, spells, and energy work differently, the following principles will give you guidance and inspiration to form your own practice as you move through this book.

A BRIEF HISTORY OF KITCHEN WITCHCRAFT

Kitchen witches have been around for centuries. Historically, for many cultures, women were traditionally the ones who did the cooking, nursing, and nurturing of the hearth and home. Therefore, kitchen witches may have been called the wisewomen, midwives, and matriarchs. These women knew how to heal a wound, deliver a baby, soothe an upset stomach, and bind a broken limb. They also knew what herbal tea to make for calming a nervous mind, which fruits to offer to the deities of love, harvest, and rain, and how to cook up whatever was available to fill hungry bellies. Kitchen witches have often been revered as holy women or leaders, and their practices and principles are present throughout history.

Today a kitchen witch looks like everyone. They can be of any age, gender, or background. And they are still the ones people come to for guidance, recipes, comfort, and healing. Whether they are self-taught or educated in traditions from elders, kitchen witches are the protectors of the generational and cultural magick handed down through stories, recipes, and crafts. Today's kitchen witches practice traditions that continue to keep the fires of hearth and home burning bright.

THE IMPORTANCE OF KITCHEN WITCHCRAFT

Kitchen witchcraft is an especially important and very potent form of magickal craft. In other types of magick or energy work, often a candle or some incense is lit and energy is sent out into the universe with the hope it hits the mark and returns to the practitioner. In kitchen witchcraft, especially in the cases where you are working with foods and recipes that will be ingested, intention is focused and outcomes are visualized into the physical food to be consumed. Food and ingredients can also be used symbolically as sympathetic magick for whatever the practitioner is hoping to glean. Because the energy is going from the witch into the food, and then the food is physically taken into the body of those who are sharing the meal, this energy becomes greatly beneficial to both the practitioner and those they choose to share the food with.

KITCHEN WITCHCRAFT
LORE & LEGEND

Myths and legends about kitchen witches can be found throughout history. Practiced mainly by women in homes and villages, this craft was not always seen as the magickal art or energetic focus it is today. In fact, it may have gone largely unnoticed, but that doesn't mean it didn't weave its way through many cultures. Lingering lore is all around you if you know what to look for. For example, the popular children's books by author Tomie dePaola feature Strega Nona (grandmother witch) often creating meals of overflowing pasta from a magick cauldron. In Germany, there is a centuries-old tradition of hanging a kitchen witch doll in your kitchen for good fortune in cooking delicious meals.

Some traditions of food magick and kitchen witchcraft were carried over from folklore into our everyday lives without us realizing it. Take, for example, the tradition of throwing rice at a newly married couple. Rice has been considered a prosperity food in many areas of the world for thousands of years. It has been associated with deities like Lakshmi, the Hindu goddess of wealth, as well as the Japanese goddess Inari. In the case of some weddings, by throwing rice, the well-wishers were seen as showering the newly married couple with prosperity magick, or so the tradition states. Even adages we might not think have roots in witchcraft might. Ever heard of winning the heart of a potential partner "through their stomach"?

CALLING IN THE NATURAL WORLD

When you call the natural world into your kitchen, you invite nature, its spirit, and its abundance to join you in your magickal work. Kitchen witchcraft allows you to do this by staying aware of the source of the food. By cooking and eating seasonally, it becomes easier to synchronize with the rhythms of what Mother Earth is providing. If farmers' markets are not an option for you, look up a website for local agriculture in your state for what is in season. You may consider investigating local community produce shares or co-ops in which you can participate for little or no cost and where you can share in the work on a farm for a portion of the harvested produce.

FOSTERING COMMUNITY & SHARED KNOWLEDGE

Nothing brings people together like a great meal. Most kitchen witches are solitary practitioners, but it also becomes a community practice because they can often share their craft with others through food. Fostering community becomes something tangible for kitchen witches because food is shareable with people of all backgrounds and beliefs, not just with other witches. All humans need food to live, so food binds us together. Whipping up a hearty soup brimming with comfort and healing energy for a friend who has suffered a loss or illness fosters connection, no matter what path that friend follows or the beliefs they hold. The magick is in the meal, the intention, and the sharing of the love through the medium of food.

THE KITCHEN WITCH'S CREED

At the core, a kitchen witch is deeply rooted in nurturing the self, home, and those they consider family. They use food, ingredients, simple spells, ancestral traditions, modern processes, and practicality to create magick. You may do that by creating gourmet meals from scratch, or by making slow cooker cauldrons or peanut butter on toast. A kitchen witch might grow herbs on a windowsill or grab some dried herbs at the dollar store when needed. No matter the spell, recipe, or tradition they follow, a kitchen witch's creed will almost always include two guiding principles. The first is to do no harm to others or yourself, which you may see a lot in your studies of witchcraft, since most modern pagans and witches take this one to heart. The second is to follow the threefold law of energy return, meaning that whatever energy you put into the universe will come back on you, times three.

TO HARM NONE

The phrase "harm none" is often called the Wiccan Rede. One way of interpreting this is to not knowingly, or unknowingly, harm another or yourself. It is paramount that you remember that to Harm None also means to do no harm to yourself. When working with energy, it's important that you consider the ramifications of your workings to keep yourself from any foreseeable physical, emotional, or psychic harm. Setting good boundaries, taking care of yourself to the best of your ability, and asking for help when needed are all things that fall under this creed. Second, it is never okay to harm others. If you begin any kind of magickal, spiritual, or energy work with the intent to harm, damage, manipulate, or in any way hurt another person, stop what you are doing and reevaluate. Harming someone with magick on purpose is never the right call.

THE THREEFOLD LAW

In recent years, there has been much talk in the media of the law of attraction, which states that any thoughts or energy you put out into the universe will come back to you. Similarly, the threefold law states that everything you put out into the universe will come back to you, times three. For example, if you knowingly enter magickal work with the intention to harm, that energy will come back to you in time and be much worse than what you put out. Likewise, if you enter energetic works with openness, trust, gratitude, and joy, these things will also return to you. Keep in mind that this return of energy rarely arrives in the form you expected and may take longer than you hoped, but the idea is simple: You get back what you put out.

THE KITCHEN IS THE HEART OF YOUR MAGICKAL PRACTICE

The kitchen is often called the heart of the home. In a traditional European home, it was the room that held the hearth–a large fireplace, usually wood-burning, that served as the center of warmth for many homes throughout history. This hearth was tended consistently during cold months and was where an entire family might sleep on long winter nights. It was also where food was cooked and where the light was best for crafting or reading. Today our modern kitchens are still gathering places: conversations happen, board games are played, tears are shed, children might do homework, and families gather. When you have a party, no matter how many great snacks you put in the living room or what's on the TV, everyone tends to gather in the kitchen.

The modern-day kitchen is also a bustling, often messy or crowded space. These traits might not seem very spiritual, but a kitchen does not have to be full of incense or crystals to be considered sacred. When you stop to think about it, magick happens in the kitchen every day. Among the piled-up dishes, spilled glasses of milk, lost keys, and dirty countertops, the kitchen is where people come to nourish their bodies and, with a little mindfulness, the space transforms into a place of sacred work.

CONCLUSION

Practices that stand the test of time are deeply rooted in who we are as human beings. You can see this in centuries of traditions of people cooking, brewing, and baking for purposes other than sating hunger. So many of these traditions endure throughout history because bonding over the preparation of food or gathering around the table to share a meal with friends and family can deepen spiritual well-being. Kitchen witchcraft traditions, specifically, can show you how to work with the natural world in season, focus your energy into food, connect more deeply to the hearth and home, and share your practice with loved ones and community.

≫ KEY TAKEAWAYS:

+ Kitchen witches have been around for centuries and can be found in every corner of the world.

+ Cooking and eating seasonally, when possible, keeps you connected to Mother Earth.

+ Gathering friends, community, and loved ones is one way kitchen witches share knowledge and their practice.

+ Setting out with the intention to Harm None is crucial for energy workers.

+ Energy you give out will come back to you in time, amplified by the power of three.

CHAPTER 3

THE KITCHEN WITCH'S CUPBOARD & PANTRY ESSENTIALS

Before you cook for a large group of people, there is a lot of planning to do. There's planning the menu, grocery shopping, cleaning the space, laying out pots and pans, preheating the oven—the list goes on and on. When readying your space for the practical magickal applications of kitchen witchcraft, it is similarly important to be prepared. With a well-equipped kitchen, a few must-haves, and a little bit of forethought, you'll be able to focus on your magickal work instead of spending time combing through your junk drawer hoping to find something that will function as a wand or whisk. Regular supplies like pots, pans, knives, jars, and spoons are as important to a kitchen witch as paintbrushes are to an artist. With a few staple items, and a little bit of planning, whipping up some magick in the kitchen can become second nature.

THE IMPORTANCE OF A WELL-EQUIPPED KITCHEN

Having the right tools and a well-equipped kitchen are of paramount importance for being able to execute the practice of kitchen witchcraft. A beautiful part of kitchen magick is that you can do it daily, and it becomes easier and simpler when you have everything you need right at your fingertips. When your tools are organized and stored in easy-to-reach places, you'll be able to grab them quickly. Similarly, in the case of food ingredients, you'll be able to see when stocks are running low. There is no need to run out and spend tons of money on new items—you probably have most of these kitchen staples already. If there are items in this chapter that you feel you need to buy new, remember that things do not need to be expensive or fancy to work the wonders of kitchen witchcraft. The cost of the object has little to do with its ability to help you in your magickal workings. It's the energy you channel with and through that object that makes the real impact.

STOCKING YOUR PANTRY

A pantry is a catchall cupboard where you can store shelf-stable items such as cereal, olive oil, crackers, pasta, nut butter, and canned goods. For a kitchen witch, a pantry, or even a large cabinet, is a treasure trove of ingredients and inspirations. Blending everyday meal prep, quick snacking, and the magickal practices of kitchen witchcraft, this space should hold dry ingredients like grains, baking supplies, and oils as well as other nonperishables. You might also store things like dried herbs, tea, and tinctures in your pantry. Always use the space available to you and put like items near one another for easy organization. For example, if you have the space, maybe one shelf in your pantry can be devoted to baking goods, grains, and rice. Be sure to read packages to ensure that something shelf-stable or canned does not need to be refrigerated once it is opened.

LEAVES & HERBS

Many kitchen witches start their journey into magick though common herbs. Dried herbs can be used for steeping tea, seasoning soups, anointing candles, burning for incense, sprinkling as garnish, and more. They can be incorporated into spellwork and healing sachets, burned in fires, and eaten for their healing or energetic properties. Some herbs, like white sage, have specific purposes within their cultures of origin and are not open to common use. So be sure to research the history, as well as the usage, for herbs you plan to incorporate into your own craft.

Herbs can be purchased pre-dried and in small jars at any grocery store, but they can also be grown in many environments. Maybe you have a sunny window in your kitchen perfect for a small parsley plant. If you grow your own herbs, be sure to dry them properly by laying them flat on a towel until no moisture remains before storing them in containers for later use. Dried herbs can last for up to two years in airtight containers.

GRAINS & POWDERS

Keeping an abundant stock of dried grains like rice, ground corn, oatmeal, and flour is another kitchen witch tradition. Energetically, these items are often associated with prosperity, friendship, and long life. But while many contemporary diets rely heavily on grains like wheat, as do numerous conventional spell recipes, that doesn't mean people with food sensitivities cannot partake. A reliable stock of gluten-free flours like rice, tapioca, and corn flour can be kept and used as substitutes in most cases for recipes, as well as for spells. Conventional and gluten-free flours, grains, and meals such as ground flaxseed are all relatively easy to find and moderately priced these days, and they are useful in whipping up magickal cakes, breads, and cookies.

PRODUCE

Produce is especially important to a kitchen witch, as it encourages connection with the earth. The magick of produce begins at the time of selection. The closer that produce is to coming out of the earth or off the vine, the more life energy it retains, and the more potent it will be in your spells and recipes. That's not to say frozen fruits and veggies are not fantastic for retaining magick and flavor. Produce can be used for its innate magickal properties, but it can also be used symbolically, based on its shape or color. Fresh produce is available in many grocery stores and farmers' markets, and some retail chains have well-priced, delicious, in-season fruits and vegetables. Whatever resources are available to you for produce, fresh or frozen, supermarket or farmers' market, the magick begins with your energy and excitement.

PROTEIN SOURCES

In kitchen witchcraft, both plant- and animal-based proteins and fats can play a significant role, often acting as a focus ingredient for channeling spellwork. For example, chicken holds energetic qualities associated with health and well-being, which is why chicken soup can be so restorative. However, there are many schools of thought around the use of animal protein. Your own practice should be guided by your personal values and dietary needs. If you choose to prepare your spells with animal products, try to do so with reverence and gratitude for the life of the animal, as well as the farmers who tended to it. If you choose to work with meat substitutes, look for those that are minimally processed. When working with such plant-based proteins, you would tap into the energetic properties of the parent plant. For example, tofu is made of soybeans, which are associated with prosperity.

EQUIPMENT & SUPPLIES

Kitchen witches need very few, if any, obscure items to whip up magick. Cauldrons, wands, and burning hearth fires are not so hard to find in their twenty-first-century iterations. Today's cauldron is a large saucepan, today's wand is a wooden spoon, today's hearth fire is a warm oven or grill, and the microwave is its own form of magick. The ritual tools of a kitchen witch are some of the most modest of kitchen instruments. Using natural materials like metal pots, glass bowls, wooden spoons, and ceramic baking dishes can help you not only cook a meal, but also participate in practical kitchen crafts. In kitchen witchcraft, many items used in everyday cooking can be put to work for the purposes of magick. When doing simple things with intention, like simmering soup or bringing a teakettle to a boil, these objects become the vessels where spells are created, rituals are celebrated, and visualizations are held.

POTS & PANS

Pots and pans are modern-day cauldrons that hold all the energy of the magick. A favorite pan gets used repeatedly because it creates the best results. It's not just that it cooks food well with even heat or crispy edges, but there is a comfort to be found in its familiarity. It amplifies your own spiritual vibrations. The stove and oven are conduits of alchemy. When you put ingredients in your favorite pan or pot to cook with heat—the element of fire—you turn that food into something more, something different, something nurturing and life providing. Pots, pans, baking dishes, mixing bowls—all of these are the vessels that hold the space for the transformation of the food to turn into something to nurture the body and soul.

COOKING UTENSILS

You will never, and I mean never, find a kitchen witch without at least one wooden spoon. A wooden spoon is at the top of the list of essential kitchen witch tools for cooking, performing rituals, and spell-casting. A wooden spoon is a kitchen witch's magick wand, in the literal sense. The spoon focuses the energy of the witch from their hand into whatever is being cooked. If you have only one tool in your kitchen witch toolbox, let it be the wooden spoon. Although silicone and plastic utensils are handy for many tasks, when working in a space of kitchen witchcraft, try to fill it with utensils made of natural elements. Wood, bamboo, and metal are all good for conducting vibrational energy.

JARS OR STORAGE CONTAINERS

There is an adage that witches love and collect jars, like crows collect shiny objects. Jars of all shapes and sizes are used by witches of all practices, but kitchen witches are known to have them stacked and packed with herbs, seeds, teas, and even spells. Glass jars with tight-fitting lids are always great for storing loose herbs or dry ingredients for cooking and magick. Jars may also be used as drinking vessels or for growing small plants. Canning or preserving is also a practice of many kitchen witches, who make jams or ferment vegetables and require clean jars and fresh lids. You'll find that jars are often used for simple rituals as well, to house a spell or to bury an intention.

TIPS FOR FINDING LOW-COST COOKWARE

You don't need to spend a lot of money on fancy equipment for your kitchen witch practice. The mindset behind your magick is the most important thing. So being resourceful, cost effective, and conscious about wastefulness are part of the overall practice. Thrift stores are wonderful places to find items like glass jars, bowls, or large metal pots and pans. Try to avoid used items that have chipped, nonstick coatings. Garage sales and online marketplaces may offer options for items like slow cookers, mixers, and blenders. If you can find a restaurant or cooking-supply shop going-out-of-business sale, you may be surprised at the high-quality cookware you can get within your budget.

When it comes to porous items like wooden spoons or cutting boards, you will want to purchase new ones only. Bacteria can grow in these items if they are not kept properly. However, large discount retailers may have excellent quality low-cost options for wooden or bamboo utensils, often offering sets of two or more for a lower price. As for jars, ask your friends and family to wash and keep any jars for you. Make sure they are cleaned well before using them for storage. Use only sterilized jars and new lids for canning or preserving.

CONCLUSION

The kitchen isn't just the place where you do magick; it's also the place that houses ingredients for inspiration into your magickal practice. It is your palette containing all the colors, textures, tastes, and flavors of the tapestry woven from food and magick. To create anything–be it art, meals, or magick–having the right tools for the job is key. For the kitchen witch, these tools start with ingredients and encompass everything from spatulas and colanders to measuring cups and whisks. You do not need to be an experienced cook; you just need to know what you have in your box of tricks and keep putting them together to create something magickal.

≫ KEY TAKEAWAYS:

+ Ingredients that are as close as possible to freshly coming out of the earth make better meals and better magick, but they do not need to be expensive or fancy.

+ Do not neglect your herbs and spices. They are an important and uncomplicated way to add energy, as well as flavor, to spells and meals.

+ When choosing ingredients, choose as locally as possible when you are able. The fresher the food, the more life force it retains.

+ Cooking is alchemy. Using tools made of natural materials helps retain and amplify your magick.

+ A wooden spoon is a kitchen witch's wand. Do not be without one.

CHAPTER 4

PREPARING YOUR KITCHEN FOR SPELLWORK

The art and practice of kitchen witchcraft comes from you—your intentions, your energy, and how you feel in the kitchen. Before any magickal workings can begin, the way you think and feel and how you approach your kitchen must be in alignment with your intentions. This space can be the busiest and most used place in the home. In this chapter, we'll explore how to shift your mindset and see your kitchen as a place where the modern world and the magickal meal-making world meet. By cleaning the space, honoring deities or ancestors (should they resonate with you), and setting up your kitchen altar, you can remind yourself of the sacredness of work that happens there—not just when you are working a specific spell, but every day. When you change the way you look at the space by creating a place of magick, love, and purpose, kitchen witch energy can flow.

CREATING SACRED SPACE IN THE KITCHEN

The first step to get your space ready for kitchen witchcraft is cleaning. Set an intention as you are cleaning by imagining all the wonderful meals and magick you are going to create. If possible, start in the corner of the room that is pointed north and work your way clockwise around the space. Remove everything from the counters to clean their surfaces. Then move on to the cabinets, disposing of any food that is past its expiration date. Before putting anything back into the cabinet, cleanse any negative energy by wafting the smoke of dried cedar or rosemary into those tight corners and neglected spaces. Negative energy collects in these areas and will settle in corners if not cleared. Apply these cleaning principles to your refrigerator and freezer, hard-to-reach spaces like above the stove, and inside the microwave. When cleaning appliances, for safety always use the proper cleaning tools and solutions suggested by the manufacturer.

If you share a kitchen with others, be sure to talk to your housemates. If they agree to you cleaning, then work around items that belong to them, doing as much as possible in communal spaces. In smaller spaces where a traditional kitchen is not present, clean any areas where food is kept or eaten. Cleaning the space with these techniques allows magickal energies to flow more readily to and through your kitchen.

THE DEITIES OF THE KITCHEN

Many cultures recognize a hearth or home deity, and all are welcome in the witch's kitchen. By adding a small statue, drawing, or image of a deity to your altar, you invite the energy of this otherworldly being to join you as you work. There are a few gods and goddesses who are most frequently invited into the kitchen. One of the best known is Brigid, Celtic goddess of the flame, who is often depicted with flowing red hair and is the keeper of the sacred hearth. Another kitchen goddess, one from Welsh tradition, is Cerridwen, who is the protector of the cauldron. Cauldrons are symbols of transformation. As kitchen witches, we recognize our pots and pans as cauldrons where we transform raw ingredients into nourishing meals. Offerings have also been and continue to be made to hearth and home gods, from the ancient Egyptian god Bes to the Chinese god Zao Jun, both of whom are believed to protect these spaces. You may consider inviting the presence of Juno, the Roman goddess who protects home and family, into your kitchen. You can also connect with your ancestors by inviting them into the kitchen the same way you would invite deities, with a photo or talisman. Should you choose to honor or call on nature spirits, faeries, the beloved dead, angels, or any other deities you work with, invite them into your kitchen through images, objects, and intentions focused on your altar.

HOW TO BUILD AN ALTAR

The altar is a focal point for energies and magickal workings. These are most commonly stationary and permanent, but you can make a portable altar with just a wooden box to house sacred objects that can be set up when you're ready to do magick. This can be particularly helpful if you're sharing house space with others. The purpose of the altar is not only to have a place to channel and focus energy, but to connect to the spiritual self and remind you of the sacred nature of the space you are in. For a kitchen witch, much of the magick is done near, rather than on, the altar. However, it is important that it is set up in a space where it is visible from most parts of the room so that it may remind you to connect back to the sacred mindfulness of cooking, eating, gratitude, and spirit.

CHOOSE A SPACE IN YOUR KITCHEN

Your kitchen altar can be as large or as small as you need it to be. To set up your altar, choose a space that is easy to see while cooking or prepping food. This can be on a windowsill, on top of the stove, or on the counter, or you can go as far as to put up a shelf or cabinet. If you are in a small, shared space, you may be able to carve out a spot inside a cabinet or even have altar items in a box that you can set up and break down when you want to use it. Start with simple items that connect you with earth, air, fire, water, and your personal spirit. Try using salt for earth, incense for air, a candle for fire, and a bowl of water for water.

ADD TALISMANS, TOTEMS, SACRED OBJECTS & MORE

Adding talismans or objects to your altar can increase the power of the space and call on different energies. You may choose to keep a chalice and an athame, or ritual knife, on your altar to symbolize the Great Rite, a ritual that represents the unity of divine male and divine female energies. You may consider adding pentacles, moons, and crystals, too. You can also put small statues of gods or goddesses or photos of ancestors on the altar. Sacred objects like bones, ashes, orbs, and scrying mirrors are all welcome, too, along with carvings or pictures of animals or nature spirits for insight or protection. Choose what resonates with you on a deep spiritual level and leave off anything that doesn't. Be sure to be respectful and conscientious about objects or symbols that may have religious or spiritual significance to other cultures.

SHAPING THE ALTAR SPACE

Because this altar is going to be in a working kitchen, you may choose to keep it small or fairly contained. Having an altar cloth is a clever idea in these cases–any piece of natural fiber fabric in a color that resonates with you can work well. Use the cloth as a template on which you can lay out your sacred items and objects. This also protects surfaces from wax drippings or damage. Choosing an altar cloth can also help you change your altar for the seasons, by using assorted colors or designs as the Wheel of the Year turns. Choosing green for spring, for example, is not only a decorative accent, but it's associated with growth, prosperity, and heart chakra energy.

LIGHTING THE ALTAR

Candles are essential to any witch's altar. They help you connect with and symbolize the element of fire and are used in multiple rituals and spells. You can use taper candles, votives, tea lights, or chime candles.

Most witches use a combination of candles and rotate them on and off the altar as needed for spells and rituals. Because candles are used for so many different magickal and energetic workings, a selection of colors, shapes, and sizes is encouraged. Having one or two tea light holders and a box of tea lights and a few votives on hand in different colors is a smart habit to get into if possible. They can be used in a pinch for quick magickal workings. Be sure that all your candles are always in fire-safe containers, and never burn candles unattended.

CREATING A
SACRED FLAME

Sacred fires are often large fires lit by communities to celebrate feasts, to focus energy, or in offering to a deity or spirit. These fires are often built and tended by many over days or even weeks. By contrast, a kitchen witch's practices are often solitary and home-based. However, the tradition of building a sacred fire can be resized and reimagined to fit your home and lifestyle. One way is by using a seven-day candle, which is a candle already encased in glass, designed to burn continuously for seven days. This can be found easily online or in most craft stores. You can light the candle with your intended pur- pose and let it burn. Your intended purpose could be for health and happiness for all those in your home, or that the meals you cook will all turn out well. Drawing pictures or symbols on the outside of the candle to charge it with your purpose or in celebration of your chosen deity is another option. If you want to keep this magickal practice going, simply light a new candle each time the previous one burns out. Tend the flame regularly by visiting it and checking in with your intention as you gaze upon it, constantly aware of the magick held within it.

GENERAL TIPS & BEST PRACTICES FOR THE KITCHEN WITCH

Even when you are not preparing a full-on gourmet dinner or performing a long ritual, you can sprinkle magick into your meals with mindfulness and intention. For example, stirring clockwise puts desired energy into your dish, while stirring counterclockwise, or widdershins, removes unwanted energy. You can draw magickal symbols like pentacles or spirals in the bottom of pots while stirring, or trace them with your finger in the bottom of baking dishes before filling them with batter. Hanging herbs like rosemary, parsley, or basil to dry can not only be a way to preserve them for later use, but it can bless your home with prosperity and peace. You can also build a ritual out of the act of washing your hands before you begin cooking. Each time you lather up before prepping a meal, envision washing your day and your troubles away. You can even create a mantra of gratitude or joy to repeat as you wash your hands, envisioning your troubles and stress going down the drain so you are ready to cook and perform kitchen magick with positive energy.

CONCLUSION

Setting up your kitchen to reflect the way you feel about the space creates an energetic container to hold your practice and create magick. This serves as a constant reminder that feeding the body and spirit are not separate from kitchen witchcraft. Creating the sacred space of the kitchen, no matter the size or shape of the space, can be magick. It is not about the space, but how you feel about the space that is key. The kitchen is just a room; the sacred is what you bring into it.

≫ KEY TAKEAWAYS:

✦ Get rid of your negative or stressful feelings about the kitchen or cooking by shifting your mindset to see the sacred in daily kitchen activities.

✦ Cleaning is key to creating space for new and positive energy. Focus on those hidden corners to clear out any old, stale energy or objects that might encumber the flow you desire.

✦ Set up your altar within the line of sight of where you will be working in the kitchen so you can stay energetically tethered to the magick of the space.

✦ Implement a few simple habits like clockwise stirring or ritual handwashing to practice witchcraft in small mindful ways every day.

PART II

EVERYDAY RECIPES, SPELLS & RITUALS FOR KITCHEN WITCHCRAFT

Welcome to part 2, where the work of kitchen witchcraft begins. As you go through these recipes, rituals, and spells, you will see how easy it is to incorporate them into your daily life. A ritual is any action done with broad intent and tends to be ceremonial in nature, whereas a spell is usually done with deep focus on a specific outcome when a need arises. Any recipe for meals can be considered either a ritual or a spell when done with purposeful intention.

Going forward, each chapter in this section will discuss rituals, spells, and recipes centered on a different theme. You are going to learn about the magickal powers of visualization and what energies can be found in common ingredients and applied to or used for multiple recipes. Using simple ingredients and basic kitchen-based magickal rituals, you will work through chapters centered on cleansing, health and healing, self-care, and love. Each recipe, spell, and ritual is a building block to starting, and growing, your practice as a kitchen witch. Get inspired to use these foods, recipes, and ideas to create magick every day.

CHAPTER 5
CLEANSING & SANCTIFYING

Earlier in this book, you learned how important cleaning the kitchen can be, especially in helping create a sacred space within the home. This chapter is all about cleansing and sanctifying the sacred spaces within the heart and mind. As these are the center of your being and the places where intention and magick live, they can sometimes get bogged down with the stresses of everyday life. Clearing out these energies then becomes an important bit of magick. The following recipes are meant to help cleanse away negativity or attract and maintain peace and positivity. Becoming more open to receiving positive energies, knowledge, and love is critical to growth as a kitchen witch. Without creating space for this growth, energies and ideas that no longer serve your highest good may linger in the heart and mind.

NEGATIVITY-BANISHING ONION SPELL

Negative energy can permeate the home and heart without anyone ever realizing it. Pressure from work, home life, finances, or relationships can bog down feelings of gratitude and joy. Life can be messy at times. From getting caught in traffic or passed up for a promotion, to something as simple as getting caught in the rain, feelings of doubt and sadness might creep in unnoticed. Because of little inconveniences of the day-to-day, residual negative energy sometimes remains stuck around one's energetic self. This goes for spaces as well. The residual tension of arguments, sad news, and hard days can live in the ether of your home.

A very easy way to clean this negative energy is a quick spell using an onion. Onions hold the power to banish negativity in a space. They absorb it, and then you can simply dispose of the onion. Onions are also fantastic at helping people shed negative vibes. For example, allowing the tears to flow is a good practice for releasing negativity, and chopping onions perfectly facilitates this. When you feel the bitter sting and your eyes begin to well up, go with it. Allow the feelings to flow out of you and let them go.

This onion spell is particularly useful after an argument or when an unwanted visitor brings pain or disruption to your home and heart. This spell is most potent when done at the waning moon for general banishing of negativity, but it can be done anytime as needed.

YOU WILL NEED:

Cutting board
Large knife
Large onion
Small plate or bowl
Black candle and holder
Matches or a lighter

1. Set out your cutting board and knife and place your onion on the cutting board.

2. Place your hands on the onion and take three deep breaths. With each exhale, send any stress and negativity you may be feeling about yourself, your situation, or others into the onion.

3. Cut the onion along the middle, horizontally to show the rings.

4. Set the cut onion on the plate and recite the following chant three times:

   I banish the bad and keep the good
   My home and heart are free of pain
   I banish the hurt that holds me back
   My home and heart are open again

5. Light the candle and set it next to the onion.

6. Let the candle burn out to seal in this spell and leave the onion out at least overnight to not only cleanse your energy but also absorb any residual energy in the space.

7. Dispose of the onion in the trash. To prevent the negativity from carrying on in other forms, do not compost or eat the onion.

PEACEFUL HOME SPELL JAR

Spell jars are a very practical way to repurpose a common kitchen tool. Any kind of glass jar will do, but mason jars work best. They are easy to find and relatively inexpensive in most craft stores and online. A spell jar is like a tiny terrarium of magick that emanates the energy and intention encapsulated within. Spell jars can be put in gardens to attract faeries, put at thresholds to ward off unwanted spirits or energy, or even put under your bed to encourage vivid dreams. They can be large or small and placed all over your home or given as gifts. This one, in particular, makes a fantastic housewarming or hostess gift for your witchy friends.

Spell jars use many tools at once by combining stones, herbs, incense, flowers, or representations of the elements. They can even be used to represent the changing seasons or to house beloved items in offering to your chosen deities or ancestors. You can make one or multiple jars. The spell jar outlined here uses sandalwood incense because of its peaceful properties, as well as stones, herbs, and spices aligned with peaceful and calming energies.

YOU WILL NEED:

Stick sandalwood incense

Matches or a lighter

Large glass jar with a tight-fitting lid (I recommend an 8-ounce jar, but you can use any size from 4-ounce to 30-ounce for this spell jar)

2 or 3 dried lavender sprigs for peaceful energy

Cinnamon stick for comfort and warmth

Piece blue agate for peace

Piece smoky quartz to soothe anxiety and create calmness

3 to 5 chamomile flowers, dried or fresh, for peace and calming energy

Pinch salt to protect the home (any salt will do, but I prefer pink Himalayan salt for this spell for its calming properties)

1. Light the incense and remove the lid from the jar.

2. Swirl the burning incense stick inside the jar, letting the vessel fill with smoke to cleanse it and charge it with peaceful energy.

3. Add the lavender, cinnamon, agate, smoky quartz, and chamomile flowers to the jar. With each item, let out a soothing breath and envision the peace and comfort you will feel in your home. See your home as a sanctuary where you can rest and rejuvenate.

4. Add the salt to protect the intentions you've put into the jar.

5. Close the lid tightly on the jar to seal in the spell.

6. Leave the jar on your kitchen altar. Repeat this process to create more jars and put one in each room if you like.

SIMPLY CLEAN KITCHEN SOLUTION— A MULTIPURPOSE CLEANER FOR YOUR SACRED SPACE

≫ MAKES 32 OUNCES OF CLEANING SOLUTION

Staying grounded in positive energy can be challenging if the space gets messy easily and is not routinely cleaned. The kitchen is your sacred space; it is a sanctuary, a temple, that you come to for meditation, magick, and meals. Keeping the space clean and tidy, on a daily basis if possible, mostly consists of cleaning up after yourself as you go while cooking, doing the dishes, and wiping down the counters. Cleaning as you go ensures your space does not get too overwhelmed with clutter or dirty dishes so that it is ready for magickal workings at any time.

What products you clean with can be as important as how often you wipe down those surfaces. Having a homemade cleaning solution that energetically aligns with your magick can help keep kitchen counters, tables, and most hard surfaces tidy between more thorough, time-consuming cleanings.

In this solution, the citrus plays a key role because its natural energetic signature is that of purification and cleansing. Adding rosemary to this solution brings a bit of calming energy, to help the home feel like a sanctuary. Note: This vinegar- and acid-based cleaner should not be used on granite or marble.

YOU WILL NEED:

Large jar with a tight-fitting lid
16 ounces filtered water
16 ounces white vinegar
1 orange
1 lemon
3 rosemary sprigs

3 drops peppermint essential oil (optional)
Small sticky paper, such as Post-it Notes
Pen

1. In a large jar or container with a tight-fitting lid, combine the water and vinegar.

2. Remove the peel from the orange using a knife, being sure to cut off only the orange peel and leaving the white pith. Repeat this step with the lemon. Reserve the fruit in an airtight container for later use.

3. As you are removing the peels from the fruit, concentrate on the image of sparkling counters. Imagine a space gleaming with joy and positive energy.

4. Combine the orange peel, lemon peel, rosemary, and peppermint oil (if using) in the container with the water and vinegar. Take your time on this step, acknowledging each ingredient as you put it into the solution.

5. Close the lid tightly and shake well.

6. Write words like "sparkle," "shine," "cleanse," and "refresh" on a few pieces of paper. Stick them to the container, letting the energy infuse into the solution as it rests for up to 7 days.

7. Pour the liquid into a spray bottle and remove the herbs and fruit peels.

8. Use on most hard surfaces around your kitchen and home.

9. Store in a cool, dark cabinet for up to 1 month.

PURELY LEMON LOAF CAKE

 MAKES 1 LOAF

Lemons are a naturally cleansing and purifying food. Like all citrus fruits, they are closely tied to sun energy and bring with them a refreshing burst of tartness or sweetness that brightens up every-thing from salads to fish. Working with lemons and other citrus is an easy way to incorporate the purification powers of these little drops of sunshine. This cake is sweet, tart, and reminiscent of a popular coffeehouse cake. While zesting the lemons, focus on their purification properties, breathe in the fresh scent deeply, and feel how it seems to brighten your senses.

YOU WILL NEED:

Nonstick cooking spray

9 x 5-inch loaf pan

Large bowl

1½ cups all-purpose flour or gluten-free all-purpose flour blend

2 teaspoons baking soda

½ teaspoon salt

Electric stand mixer or hand mixer

3 large eggs

1 cup granulated sugar

1 cup plain or vanilla yogurt

2 teaspoons lemon extract

½ cup vegetable oil

Grated zest of 3 lemons

FOR THE GLAZE

1 cup powdered sugar

1 tablespoon lemon juice

1. Preheat the oven to 350°F.

2. Apply nonstick cooking spray to the loaf pan

3. With your index finger, draw a sun in the pan. If you want to bring joy, draw your sun with a smiling face inside.

4. In a large bowl, sift together the flour, baking soda, and salt. Set aside.

5. In the bowl of a stand mixer (use a large bowl and a hand mixer if you do not have a stand mixer), combine the eggs and sugar. Mix on medium speed until fully incorporated.

6. Add the yogurt and lemon extract and continue blending on medium speed until mixed well.

7. With the mixer running on medium speed, slowly pour in the oil until fully incorporated.

8. Turn off the mixer and slowly mix in the lemon zest by hand.

9. Pour the batter into the prepared loaf pan and bake on the middle rack for 50 to 55 minutes. Test the loaf by inserting a toothpick in the center. When it comes out clean, the loaf is done.

10. Let the loaf cool completely after removing it from the oven. When it is completely cool and no longer warm to the touch, remove it from the pan and set it on a serving dish or tray lined with parchment paper.

11. Make the glaze by combining the powdered sugar and lemon juice and mix gently until consistency is smooth and it easily drizzles from the spoon. Add more lemon juice, if needed, for the proper consistency.

12. Drizzle the glaze on top of the cooled loaf.

13. Slice and enjoy. Store in an airtight container for up to a week.

REFRESHING GRAPEFRUIT SALAD

>> SERVES 4—THE RECIPE CAN BE CUT IN HALF FOR SMALLER SERVINGS IF DESIRED.

Salads can be a kitchen witch's masterpiece, when done right. And they can be made and shared for most occasions. You can use many different ingredients in endless combinations for almost any energetic or magickal work. They can be made for large groups or for just one person's enjoyment, and can be a side or a complete meal. Salads are easy to toss together and even easier to enjoy at any time of the year.

The kitchen witchcraft that can exist in a salad is so special because the ingredients change with every subtle shift in the season. In early spring, you could make a salad to celebrate the season with asparagus, baby peas, and fresh goat cheese. Or in autumn, a salad can bring together apples, walnuts, and bitter greens in honor of the coming winter.

In the case of the following salad recipe, you are going to throw together a few ingredients to refresh and renew spirits. Grapefruit holds the power of cleansing and purification like all citrus fruits. When combined in this salad with the sharp licorice bite of fennel, the flavor and the energies work together to create something truly magickal. Fennel in all its forms–seed, bulb, and flower–has associations with love and protection magick.

YOU WILL NEED:

8 ounces arugula
8 ounces baby spinach
1 cup shaved fennel bulb

1 large red grapefruit
½ red onion, thinly sliced
½ cup feta cheese (optional)

FOR THE DRESSING

½ cup extra-virgin olive oil
¼ cup water
¼ cup white wine vinegar
Juice of ½ grapefruit
1 tablespoon sugar

1 teaspoon dried oregano
1 teaspoon dried basil
Salt
Freshly ground black pepper

1. In a large bowl, toss together the arugula, spinach, and fennel. Set aside.

2. Cut the grapefruit into supremes by cutting in half lengthwise, then, using a small paring knife, cutting the fruit sections away from the delicate skin and separating it from the rind. Place the grapefruit supremes in a bowl and set aside.

3. Make the dressing by combining the oil, water, vinegar, grapefruit juice, sugar, oregano, basil, and salt and pepper to taste in a large bowl and whisking together.

4. Delicately place the grapefruit supremes on top of the greens, then sprinkle on the red onion.

5. Toss lightly with the dressing, adding more by the tablespoon until the salad is evenly coated to your taste.

6. While tossing the salad, recite the following mantra: *My health, wealth, love, and life are refreshed by the power of my will, so mote it be!*

7. Sprinkle with feta cheese (if using) and serve immediately.

CHAPTER 6

HEALTH & HEALING

Supporting others and the self with general health and wellness is central to what kitchen witches do. A great deal of basic kitchen witchcraft focuses on health and healing because traditional remedies used to be made in the home. Before the invention of antinausea medication sold over the counter at the pharmacy, a local wise woman or herbalist might have recommended peppermint tea. Likewise, if someone was suffering from a broken heart, the same practitioner might have suggested to make a sachet of rose petals to keep around their neck to soothe the emotional wound. This chapter has some go-to recipes and spells for overall wellness. These are things that can be made over and over throughout the year and, in some cases, they can be stored and used all year long. Please note, the following recipes are not meant to cure illness. If you are suffering from any ailments–physical, emotional, or mental–please seek professional opinions.

FIRE CIDER SPELL

>> MAKES 32 OUNCES

Fire cider is a traditional herbal remedy for boosting immune response. Fresh ingredients are key in this recipe for potency. Do not use dried, jarred, or precut ingredients. This recipe is accompanied by a spell that encapsulates the healing powers of the ingredients. Fire cider can be taken by the tablespoonful, straight out of the bottle, but is more palatable if you mix a tablespoon or two with hot water and honey for a warm drink. Make this cider during the waxing moon to draw in good health.

YOU WILL NEED:

Large (32-ounce, at least) glass jar with a tight-fitting lid
1 cup chopped red onion
3 garlic cloves, chopped
4 ounces fresh turmeric, chopped
4 ounces fresh ginger, chopped

1 whole lemon, chopped (skin on)
1 whole orange, chopped (skin on)
1 whole chile, such as jalapeño or habanero, chopped
4 cups raw apple cider vinegar

1. Prepare your large jar by making sure it is washed and fully dried before starting this recipe.

2. With all your ingredients prepped, take a deep cleansing breath and visualize yourself feeling strong and healthy. Envision a warm sunbeam from the center of your chest radiating down your arms as you begin to put each ingredient in your jar.

3. Recite the following incantations as you put each ingredient in the jar, holding it in your hands as you speak the words out loud:

I call upon the banishing power of onion to keep me free of illness
I call upon the protective power of garlic to keep me safe from harm
I call upon the power of turmeric to keep my body moving freely
I call upon the power of ginger to keep my digestion smooth
I call upon the cleansing power of lemon to keep my body clean

I call upon the power of orange to keep my immune system healthy
I call upon the power of peppers to fill me with the fire and energy
of the sun

4. Pour the apple cider vinegar over the ingredients, making sure the liquid covers everything. If you need to add more vinegar to cover the ingredients, do so now.

5. Close the lid tightly. Shake the jar vigorously and place in a warm spot in the kitchen, preferably where it can sit in the sun.

6. After a week of it sitting in the sun, strain the liquid through a sieve and pour it into a clean jar or bottle. At this point, you may add honey to sweeten the cider if you wish.

7. Store in a cool, dry place for up to 6 months. Drink 1 or 2 tablespoons daily to boost the immune system or take to lessen the effects of a cold at the onset of symptoms.

BREATHE DEEP SIMMER POT

>> MAKES 1 LARGE SIMMER POT

Simmer pots are deliciously scented pots of fragrant ingredients that can be used for aromatherapy or adding moisture to the air. They are not only easy to make but also can be turned into a ritual with just a little intuition and a few extra steps. The following is a simmer pot for helping you breathe deeper. It will not only help you physically take a deeper breath by opening your sinuses and filling your lungs with warm, moist air, but it will also help you slow down and focus on your life-giving breath.

You will want to check on your pot about every hour or so, and if you want to keep it going for longer, just add more water. Once you know how to make a simmer pot, you can try other ingredients for the energies you might like. For example, you can toss in some lemons for purification, apples for blessing, or pine for connecting with nature. Think of seasonal scents and try many different combinations.

YOU WILL NEED:

Large (4- or 5-quart) pot
2 large oranges, cut into rounds
Handful whole cloves
2 or 3 eucalyptus sprigs
2 or 3 peppermint sprigs
2 or 3 rosemary sprigs
3 cinnamon sticks

1. Fill the pot about three-quarters of the way with water.

2. Place the pot on the stove.

3. Add all the other ingredients to the pot.

4. Turn the stove to medium-high heat and wait for the water to come to a boil.

5. Take a comfortable seat in the kitchen as you wait. Sit facing your stove if you can. Put your hands in your lap, palms facing up.

6. Take deep breaths in and out, focusing on how the air fills your lungs. Continue to do this until you hear the gentle bubble of the simmer pot and start to smell it releasing fragrance.

7. Once it comes to a boil, turn down the heat to a simmer.

8. Stand over the pot and deeply breathe in the steam coming from the pot. Notice the scents and how the warm, moist air is filling your nose, sinuses, and lungs. Take three to five deep breaths from the pot before moving on with your day.

9. Set a timer for every 60 minutes to check on your simmer pot. Continue adding water to the pot if you want to keep the scent lingering longer or if you want to come back for five more breaths over the course of a few hours. Never leave the stove on if you exit the house.

BE WELL TEA

≫ MAKES 2 CUPS LOOSE-LEAF TEA

Herbal tea, a staple in the homes of many kitchen witches, is any tea that is not made with tea leaves, either black or green, and is not caffeinated. The magickal correspondences of herbs, specifically those that are brewed for tea, can be as varied as the flavor combinations you can achieve by making your own blends. Working with herbs requires some basic knowledge of plants and their purposes. For example, if you are feeling anxious, you might reach for a warm soothing cup of chamomile, or, if you have an upset stomach, maybe a piping-hot mug of peppermint tea. In any case, creating herbal tea blends can be fun and filled with magick when you deeply connect with the energies and wellness qualities of the herbs.

All the herbs in this tea are easy to find. However, you'll need to make sure they are suitable for consumption. In some cases, herbs are grown for burning or crafting and can be treated with chemicals or toxins for preservation, which makes them unsafe for consumption. Ask the shop owner or look online for herbs and spices meant for tea.

This tea features another antioxidant champion, the elderberry. It also has eucalyptus for anti-inflammation, peppermint to soothe the tummy, and chamomile to help you rest. The taste of this tea is grassy and can be bitter. Keeping that in mind, you may want to add more peppermint, or make your cup with honey for sweetness. All in all, this tea is a perfect tonic when you are not feeling well or to keep up your general wellness. Making a big batch of this loose tea and storing for the season is a great practice to get into in the fall as the weather turns chilly. Mixing this tea together in preparation for the winter months may be a fun tradition around Samhain, October 31, and the start of the winter season. There's more on Samhain in chapter 11.

YOU WILL NEED:

¼ cup dried stinging nettle leaf
½ cup dried peppermint leaf
¼ cup dried eucalyptus

¼ cup dried elderberries
¼ cup chamomile

1. In a large bowl, combine all the ingredients.

2. Gently mix or toss with a wooden spoon, being careful not to crush the leaves too much.

3. Remove the loose herbal mixture into an airtight container and store for up to a year.

4. To make a cup of tea, put a tablespoon of herbal mixture in a tea strainer or loose-leaf tea bag.

5. Pour 8 to 10 ounces of boiling water over the tea bag and let it steep for no longer than 5 minutes.

6. Remove the tea bag and sweeten with raw, unfiltered honey if desired.

A KITCHEN WITCH'S CURE-ALL CHICKEN SOUP

≫ SERVES 6 TO 8

A bubbling pot of chicken soup speaks to the very heart of a kitchen witch's soul. The magickal healing properties of chicken soup are not just felt by the person eating it, but also by the person making it. And those healing properties are not merely old wives' tales or superstitions. There is scientific evidence showing that when chicken bones are boiled for broth, they release all kinds of wonderful nutrients that are good for our bodies. Magickally speaking, the energy of chicken is for health and well-being. When you simmer, stir, and simmer again, the magick of this soup takes form. By pouring your intentions for health and well-being for all who will enjoy this meal, you are infusing the soup with those energies. Be clear about the type of comfort you hope this soup imparts on the intended person. Visualize yourself or them being warmed from the inside out with every bite. As the person making this soup, feel joyful and let that joy fill your heart, as the soup will fill the body of whoever eats it.

Chicken soup can be made from scratch, or semi-scratch as many would call it. You can, of course, take the long road of baking a chicken, deboning it, boiling the bones for broth, and using the meat for the soup. Though this recipe is going to call for boxed broth and leftover or store-bought rotisserie chicken to save time, it may be more practical kitchen witchcraft, but no less magickal.

YOU WILL NEED:

Large (5-quart) sauce pot
2 tablespoons olive oil
1 cup chopped celery
1 yellow onion, chopped
1 cup chopped carrots
3 garlic cloves, minced

2 (32-ounce) cartons chicken bone broth (organic is preferable)
2 cups cubed cooked chicken
Salt
Freshly ground black pepper
Rosemary sprigs

1. In the sauce pot, warm the oil over medium heat.

2. Add the celery, onion, carrots, and garlic.

3. Cook, sautéing on medium heat until the onions are soft and translucent.

4. Add the chicken broth and chicken.

5. Bring to a boil.

6. Once boiling, add salt and pepper to taste and stir three times, clockwise to infuse the soup with positive intentions for health and healing.

7. Reduce the heat to a simmer.

8. Add the rosemary on top of the liquid and cover the pot.

9. Let soup simmer on low heat for at least 1 hour.

10. Serve hot with noodles or crusty bread for dipping.

CALM YOUR COCONUT CURRY

>>> SERVES 4 TO 6

Health and well-being are not all about tending to sickness or trying to avoid a cold. Finding a calming center is also important to overall wellness. Calming the mind is challenging for many people who have busy lives. Finding a moment to trade feelings of being overwhelmed for feelings of relaxation and mindfulness is something to strive for and will keep your practice of creating magick in the kitchen centered in the work you are doing. When you combine coconut milk with chicken for health and red curry paste for fire energy, this dish brings soothing energy to feelings of being frazzled.

Certain foods can help with focus and grounding. Coconut, for example, has the properties to cool, calm, and rejuvenate. Therefore, it is the key magickal ingredient in this curry dish. Coconut's energy is synonymous with nourishing, soothing, and the full moon. Use canned full-fat coconut milk here—if you use a low-fat version, it will not have the right consistency. Be sure to shake the can well before opening and pouring out the coconut milk, as it tends to harden in the can and will not pour properly if you do not shake it. You can easily make this dish vegetarian if you omit the chicken and add more vegetables, such as broccoli, green peppers, or snap peas in step 3, and simply skip to step 5.

YOU WILL NEED:

2 pounds chicken thighs cut into 1-inch cubes
Salt
Freshly ground black pepper
Large skillet
2 tablespoons olive oil
1 large onion, sliced
1 large red bell pepper, sliced

1 (15-ounce) can full-fat coconut milk, shaken well
1 tablespoon fish sauce
1 or 2 teaspoons red curry paste
2 cups cooked rice
Chopped fresh cilantro for garnish (optional)

1. Sprinkle the chicken with salt and pepper to taste and set aside while you prepare your other ingredients.

2. In the skillet over medium-high heat, warm the oil.

3. Add the onion and bell pepper to the skillet and cook until they are just starting to soften, about 3 minutes.

4. Add the chicken, sautéing it until cooked through.

5. Add the coconut milk, fish sauce, and red curry paste. Bring it to a low boil, stirring occasionally.

6. Lower the heat to let the liquid simmer and thicken, about 20 minutes.

7. Spoon over cooked rice and enjoy warm topped with cilantro (if using).

CHAPTER 7

SELF-CARE & VIBRANCY

Self-care is not selfish. Self-care is a key component of being a kitchen witch. Because so much of kitchen witchcraft is focused on nurturing others through the crafts of food magick and intention in cooking, it is important that you are also taking care of and nurturing yourself. Before you can give your energy to the work of taking care of others, you must first take care of yourself to be able to be fully vibrant and present. As the adage of self-care goes: *You cannot pour from an empty cup.* Therefore, using specific recipes, ingredients, and rituals for loving the self and keeping your vibrant spark is vital to the practice of kitchen witchcraft. This chapter will address self-care and self-love through a ritual bath made with herbs from your kitchen, meals that will ignite a spark to keep your energy glowing, and an incredible sleep tincture for restful nights.

LOVING SELF INFUSED RITUAL BATH SALT

Self-care often starts with calming the mind and releasing tension. For these reasons, a warm, soothing soak can be beneficial to the mind and body. Bath salts require little more than a few ingredients from your kitchen cupboards and are usually made at the kitchen altar. This is a reminder of how kitchen witchcraft can transfer from one part of your home to another.

The following ritual infuses bath salt with ingredients for loving the self, such as rose petals and antianxiety dried passionflowers. Do *not* use regular table salt, as it could irritate or dry the skin, whereas Epsom salt and sea salt have nutrients that are thought to relax muscles and soothe irritation when dissolved in warm water.

YOU WILL NEED:

3 cups plain Epsom salt

1 cup coarse salt, such as Himalayan pink salt

¼ cup baking soda

2 tablespoons dried rose petals

2 tablespoons dried passionflower

Large (32-ounce) jar with a breathable lid

Toothpick or pin

Pink candle and holder

White candle and holder

Light blue candle and holder

Lavender candle and holder

Rose quartz crystal, for loving the self

Moonstone crystal, for renewal of spirit

Blue lace agate crystal, for self-esteem

Amethyst crystal, for serenity

Matches or a lighter

1. Make the bath salt.
   A. In a large bowl, mix together the Epsom salt, coarse salt, baking soda, dried roses, and dried passionflower.
   B. Transfer the prepared bath salt to a jar with a breathable lid. Poke holes in the lid or use a lid that is vented to ensure that gases from the baking soda do not build up and cause the jar to crack.

2. Using the toothpick or pin, carve the following words into the candles.
   A. "SELF-LOVE" into the pink candle
   B. "RENEWAL" into the white candle
   C. "SELF-ESTEEM" into the blue candle
   D. "SERENITY" into the lavender candle

3. Set each candle on the kitchen altar in a circle with its coordinating stone next to it: pink candle with rose quartz, white with moonstone, blue with blue lace agate, and lavender with the amethyst.

4. Place the jar of bath salt in the middle of the circle of candles.

5. Light each candle in the circle. Visualize the words carved on each as a beam of warm candlelight infusing into the bath salt.

6. Allow the candles to burn down before removing the jar of bath salt. The ritual is complete when the candles burn down.

7. Fill the bathtub with warm water and add 2 or 3 tablespoons of bath salt. Place each one of the crystals from the ritual around the tub while you bathe, relax, and renew in the healing water of your bathtub.

8. Store the remaining bath salt in a cool, dry place for up to 3 months.

SOUND SLEEP TINCTURE

Sleep is vital to existence. Without proper sleep, the human body, mind, and spirit cannot function properly. Poor sleep can affect everything from mood to judgment and physical well-being. The body needs proper rest to restore itself from daily activities and to recharge and renew for another day. Getting a good night's sleep regularly is imperative self-care that keeps you vibrant and alert in all your daily activities.

The following tincture uses herbs and alcohol to help you fall asleep and stay asleep longer. A tincture is a solution or herbal infusion concentrated into alcohol that can be taken by mouth via a dropper. Tinctures can also be made with water but will not have as much shelf stability as the alcohol-based ones. Start with a mild-flavored, clear alcohol that is at least 80 proof, like vodka. In many cases, a few drops under the tongue is enough to get the benefits of the tincture, but if you are sensitive to the taste, it's fine to dilute a few drops into water or tea. Since this tincture takes a full month to infuse, start the brewing process during the dark moon so that the energy of this spell is aligned with new beginnings. Note: Consult with your doctor or health care provider if you are pregnant, nursing, or have other medical conditions before taking any herbal remedies.

YOU WILL NEED:

¼ cup dried valerian root
¼ cup dried chamomile
¼ cup dried lavender flowers
¼ cup dried lemon balm
Large (32-ounce) jar with a
    tight-fitting lid

3 cups 80-proof plain vodka
Large piece cheesecloth or a
    fine-mesh sieve
12 2-ounce or 6 4-ounce glass
    dropper bottles with lids and
    1-milliliter droppers

1. Put all the dry herbs into the jar.

2. Cover the herbs completely with the vodka. If herbs are still partially dry or if there is room left in the jar, use more vodka to fill accordingly.

3. Cover the jar tightly.

4. Holding the jar in your hands, recite the following incantation three times:

   Restful sleep, peaceful dreams
   Restore my days, rejuvenate my life
   Restful sleep, peaceful dreams
   Restore my body, rejuvenate my mind

5. Place the jar in a sunny spot in the kitchen and let it rest for 4 weeks, shaking it once daily while reciting the incantation above.

6. After the 4 weeks have passed, strain the tincture through the cheesecloth or sieve. Be sure to squeeze all the liquid out of the herbs.

7. Pour the liquid into the dropper bottles. Seal and store at room temperature for up to 2 years.

8. Take about 1 milliliter of tincture under the tongue and hold for 60 seconds before swallowing or dilute in water or tea at bedtime.

GREEN GODDESS SALAD DRESSING

Avocados have gained popularity in recent years as a topping on toast or sandwiches. With their creamy, nutty flavor, they are full of good monounsaturated fats like those found in coconut oil and olive oil. These tasty green fruits are native to Mexico and were brought into North America in the late 1800s. They became more widely available commercially by the late 1950s. Today, avocados can be found in most commercial grocery stores and on restaurant menus all over the United States.

Avocados hold within them the energy of self-love. The beautiful green flesh of the avocado is only visible when the outer layer of skin is removed. This reminds us to see the beauty within ourselves and others. Adding avocados to sandwiches, salads, or smoothies can allow you to see the beauty within yourself. By preparing avocados with the intention to see and understand that there is beauty within yourself, you can awaken this feeling and shine your inner beauty through your physical being. The salad dressing here can be used over your favorite salad or as a dip for vegetables. Each time you enjoy it, be reminded to let the beauty within you shine out to all those around you.

YOU WILL NEED:

¼ cup olive oil
½ cup white vinegar
2 tablespoons water
1 teaspoon honey
Juice of ½ lime or lemon
Fresh cilantro or parsley

Electric blender
1 whole avocado
Toothpick or sharp knife
Salt
Freshly ground black pepper
Airtight container or bottle

1. Put the oil, vinegar, water, honey, and lime juice and cilantro to taste into the blender.

2. Cut the avocado in half lengthwise. Remove the center pit.

3. Using the toothpick or the tip of a sharp knife, write the words "I AM BEAUTIFUL" in the flesh of the avocado.

4. As you do this, imagine that every person you come into contact with can see the beauty within your heart and that you can see theirs.

5. Using a spoon, scoop the flesh of the avocado out of the skin and into the blender.

6. Add salt and pepper to taste.

7. Blend on medium speed until smooth and creamy, adding water by the teaspoonful if the mixture is too thick.

8. Pour dressing into an airtight container and store, refrigerated, for up to 1 week.

VIBRANT VEGGIE WRAP WITH WHITE BEAN SPREAD

>>> MAKES 4 WRAPS

A large part of the practice of kitchen witchcraft is to take care of the physical body. Earlier in this book, you learned that eating in-season foods helps you stay connected to the rhythms of the earth. This idea is specifically useful when plant-based meals are the order of the day. Plants make up over 80 percent of the food consumed on our planet. Fruits, vegetables, grains, leaves, and roots are all important ingredients that help sustain life and health. Increasing the number of fresh fruits and vegetables in your diet when possible can help you feel bright and alert in mind, body, and spirit. Many witches have their own gardens or frequent farmers' markets for seasonal and affordable produce.

The magick of this recipe comes from the vegetables. You can try making it in many variations with different seasonal vegetables—for example, you can make it with roasted sweet potatoes and beets in the fall and winter months. The recipe found here is filled with springtime vegetables teeming with the new life energy of the season to create a vibrancy in the heart and mind.

YOU WILL NEED:

- 2 cups chopped asparagus
- 2 cups snap peas
- Electric blender or food processor
- 1 (15-ounce) can white cannellini beans
- 2 garlic cloves
- Juice of ½ lemon, plus more for drizzling
- 2 ounces goat cheese
- 1 tablespoon fresh dill
- 1 tablespoon fresh parsley
- 1 tablespoon olive oil, plus more for drizzling
- Salt
- Freshly ground black pepper
- 4 large wraps (10-inch works best)
- 1 large cucumber, sliced
- 1 cup baby arugula
- Large skillet
- Cooking spray

1. Blanch the asparagus and peas. Bring 3 quarts of water to a boil. Add the asparagus and peas and gently boil for 1 or 2 minutes.

2. Remove from the heat and immediately drain and soak in cold water for 5 minutes.

3. Remove from the cold water and set aside on a paper towel to dry.

4. Make the bean spread.
   A. In a blender or food processor, combine the beans and liquid from the can, the garlic, lemon juice, goat cheese, dill, parsley, oil, and salt and pepper to taste. Blend on medium speed.
   B. Remove to a medium bowl and set aside.

5. Place a single wrap on a clean work surface.

6. Spread about 2 tablespoons of bean mixture onto the center of the wrap.

7. Layer with blanched asparagus, snap peas, cucumber, and arugula.

8. Drizzle with fresh lemon juice and olive oil.

9. Fold the sides of the wrap inward and roll tightly. Repeat with remaining ingredients.

10. Heat a skillet on medium heat and spray with cooking spray.

11. Place each wrap on the warm skillet and toast until just warm on both sides, about 2 minutes.

GOLDEN GLOW SMOOTHIE

⧓⧓⧓⧓⧓⧓⧓⧓⧓⧓⧓⧓⧓⧓⧓⧓⧓⧓⧓⧓⧓⧓⧓⧓⧓⧓⧓⧓⧓⧓⧓⧓⧓⧓⧓

≫ MAKES ABOUT 24 OUNCES

A basic kitchen witch trick to starting your day right is to begin with a smoothie like this one, which helps you take your golden glow with you throughout the day. This smoothie, when made with visualization and intention, creates a dome of light around you where you are firmly rooted and empowered to be yourself. In this dome of light, you can feel completely at home with yourself, your body, and the power of your own will. It combines bright, tart, sweet mango and warm spices like cardamom and cinnamon with a kick of pepper to bring in a little fire energy. When the energies of these spices meet the soothing coconut milk, the result is a flavor that tastes like pure sunshine. Of course, you can use almond milk or oat milk if you prefer. As you add the ingredients into the blender, envision your senses waking up. Imagine being awake and aware of all the light, life, and vibrations around you, standing in a bubble of the power of your own will and intention as you move through your day. The spices in the recipe really hold the power of your intentions, so be specific in your visualizations. For variations on this smoothie, try adding a half cup of pineapple for a more tropical flavor or decrease the amount of liquid for a thicker smoothie that can be topped with toasted nuts or dried fruit for a smoothie bowl.

YOU WILL NEED:

12 ounces coconut, almond, or oat milk
Electric blender
1 cup frozen mango chunks
½ banana
½ cup ice cubes
2 tablespoons raw honey or agave nectar, for sweetness

¼ teaspoon ground cinnamon, for comfort
Pinch ground cardamom, for sensuality
Pinch ground turmeric, for purification
Pinch freshly ground black pepper, for fire energy
Pinch ground ginger, for love

1. Pour the milk into the blender.

2. Add the mangos and banana, then add the ice cubes.

3. Add the honey while envisioning the sweetness you'd like to carry into your day.

4. Add the cinnamon while envisioning the comfort of self-confidence.

5. Add the cardamom while envisioning the feeling of being sensual and empowered.

6. Add the turmeric while envisioning all that does not serve you melting away.

7. Add the black pepper while envisioning the warmth of the sun all around you.

8. Add the ginger while envisioning the love you wish to receive and give to the world.

9. Blend on medium speed until smooth and thick.

10. Pour into a large glass and drink immediately.

CHAPTER 8
LOVE & INTIMACY

Many recipes and ingredients are associated with giving, receiving, or rekindling love. Such foods and recipes cover a variety of feelings and can be used in many ways. It is the kitchen witch's own intention and visualization that can turn an ingredient like tomatoes, which have long been associated with love magick, into a recipe or meal to attract romance or to intensify the love between friends. In this chapter, you will briefly explore a few quintessential foods that can help bridge the gaps in long-standing relationships, attract new romance, increase intimacy, and help you fall in love with your empowered self. All gender and sexual identities are welcome and invited to these practices.

When doing any kind of magick or energy work that involves another person, be very careful that your intent is for the good of all involved and respectful of the will and boundaries of others. You must remain clear and open in your own mind and heart; otherwise the power of your spell, ritual, or recipe could be contorted by selfish or toxic energy. This type of magick is never about changing someone's opinions. If you are trying to attract love with a new partner and you have someone specific in mind, be sure this person is interested and available. If you are working to enhance or rekindle an existing relationship, having your partner's consent to do this energy work is essential.

FEEDING THE HEART RITUAL

This ritual can be done to connect with a partner or to connect more deeply to what you love about yourself. Feeding the loving feelings and focusing on the good in your partner, or in yourself, allows you to look past what might be perceived as minor imperfections to see what is clearly wonderful about the individual. This is a very intimate ritual and may cause emotions to come up to the surface. Grapes allow dreams and emotions to come forward, and so they may give you a "dreamy" energy as you work through this ritual. Be sure you have the time to tend to any emotional needs that may arise.

YOU WILL NEED:

Blanket or towel large enough for two people to sit on
Large red pillar candle and a plate to put it on
Bowl red grapes

Stick rose incense, to encourage romance
Incense holder
Matches or a lighter

1. Place the blanket on the floor in the center of the kitchen.

2. Dim the lights in the room.

3. Place the plate with the candle on it in the center of the blanket, as well as the grapes and incense and holder.

4. Sit cross-legged facing your partner. If you are doing this on your own, do your best to face a reflective surface such as a mirror or even a shiny appliance.

5. Sit as close to your partner as possible, so that you can put your hands on each other's knees, leaving room for the candle and the bowl of grapes between you.

6. Close your eyes and take three deep breaths to center yourself and clear your mind.

7. Open your eyes and light the candle and the incense.

8. Connect with your partner and gaze into each other's eyes for at least 30 seconds. This may become awkward, and you may feel the urge to laugh or look away. Do not look away. It is okay to call out the awkwardness, giggle, or shift your weight. But maintain eye contact. If you are doing this on your own, look deep into your own eyes in your reflection.

9. Take a grape from the bowl and name something you love or are grateful for about the person you are facing. It can be as simple as saying you love their smile or that you're grateful they took out the trash.

10. Feed each other grapes back and forth. Preceding each grape, give a compliment or something you are grateful for about the other. Do the same for yourself if you are doing this as a solo ritual.

11. Continue this ritual until all the grapes are gone and the incense is done burning.

12. When you are finished, keep the red candle on your kitchen altar and burn it whenever you are cooking a meal for, or with, your partner or for yourself. Let it remind you of all the things you love about each other.

PERFECTLY YOU—APRON ADORNMENT SPELL

Any garment or adornment that a witch wears while making magick or working their craft can be considered ritual attire. Some choose to wear robes of all sizes and colors for large rituals. Others prefer crowns of flowers, braided cords, or masks. A kitchen witch's signature ritual attire is an apron. Though it is not necessary to wear an apron when preparing meals throughout the day, a ritual apron can be something more than a way to keep your clothes free of spatter and food residue. It can be a spell within itself, holding the magick of your intention that you wrap around your body. When you put on your ritual apron, it is a reminder that the work of kitchen witchcraft is sacred. The following spell helps turn a humble apron into witchy garb for magickal workings. When you imbue this apron with sacred symbols and affirmations of self-acceptance and body positivity, this energy is held near your heart center whenever it is worn. Feeling comfortable and confident in your body creates personal empowerment fueled by compassion and gratitude for the beautiful body that houses your beautiful heart.

YOU WILL NEED:

Plain black apron

Fabric markers in gold, silver, and white. Other colors are acceptable as well but these three are a must: gold for solar energy, silver for lunar energy, and white to show clear intentions.

Comfortable seat at your kitchen table or wherever meals are made and food is shared

1. Lay the apron flat on the table.

2. Using the fabric markers, draw symbols on the apron that hold meaning and magick for you. Some symbols to try are: the pentacle, a five-pointed star within a circle symbolizing earth, air,

fire, water, and the human spirit working together in harmony; a moon in three phases to symbolize the goddess; or sacred spirals to symbolize the cycles of life. Use the gold marker for any solar or powerful imagery like the sun, which symbolizes masculine god energy, or trees for nature. Use the silver for any lunar imagery like moons or goddess symbols. Images and drawings of animals, flowers, or herbs can also be incorporated into any design you like for your apron. Decorate your apron with words, phrases, and imagery that mean something magickal to you.

3. As you draw these symbols on the outside of your apron, imbue your intent to do magickal workings while wearing this garment into the symbols.

4. When you are done drawing the symbols, take your apron with you to a room where you can remove your clothes and see yourself in a mirror.

5. Undress completely and put on your sacred apron.

6. Stand in front of the mirror and say the following mantra 13 times:

   I am beautiful
   I am enough
   I am perfectly me

7. When you are done, dress again and return to the kitchen.

8. Using your white marker, write the above mantra on the *inside* of the apron at the center where it will sit over your heart.

9. Keep your apron in a safe space where you can find it easily. Wear it when doing any or all magick in the kitchen, particularly magick for love and relationships.

HAPPILY EVER AFTER CHOCOLATE STRAWBERRIES

>> MAKES 12 CHOCOLATE-COVERED STRAWBERRIES

Chocolate is an ultimate love food. On the list of aphrodisiacs, it's at the top. Chocolate has a centuries-old reputation for being a food synonymous with arousal and desire, even dating back to ancient Aztec society when it was first recorded as being consumed for sexual arousal. Hot cups of cacao were said to have been shared by brides and grooms during marriage ceremonies of the Mayans, which may be the roots of our modern ideas of chocolate and romance going together.

Today, chocolate is still a decadent treat that is eaten, enjoyed, and savored for pleasure. The folklore and mythology around chocolate as an aphrodisiac have, in fact, created an energy around the substance that brings the myth to life. Likewise, strawberries are associated with romance and are often depicted as a sensual food. Having a shape that's reminiscent of a heart certainly helps their place in the hierarchy of love foods, but it is their association with Venus–the planet that rules over love and relationships–that gives them an energetic boost for amping up romance. This decadent dessert is best made with, or for, an intended lover to incite romance.

YOU WILL NEED:

12 large strawberries
Parchment paper
Large baking sheet
Decorative sprinkles in red or pink,
   the colors of love and passion

16 ounces dark chocolate,
   chopped
Microwave-safe bowl
Digital thermometer

1. Gently wash the strawberries. Keep the stems intact and dry them thoroughly but gently on a paper towel. Set aside until ready to use.

2. Cut parchment paper to fit the baking sheet and set aside.

3. Fill a shallow dish with pink decorative sprinkles and set aside.

4. Put about half the chopped chocolate in the microwave-safe bowl.

5. Heat in 30-second intervals, stirring between each heating, until melted and smooth.

6. Test the temperature of your chocolate to be sure it is not hotter than 105°F.

7. Add the remaining chocolate to the melted chocolate by the spoonful, stirring in between each addition to make sure everything is melted before adding more.

8. When all the chocolate has been added and melted, test the temperature again. When the temperature is between 85 and 90°F, begin dipping your strawberries.

9. Gently holding the strawberry by the stem, dip it in the warm chocolate, being sure to cover all sides with a thin layer.

10. Roll one side in pink decorative sprinkles.

11. Set the coated strawberry on the parchment-lined sheet and repeat the process with the remaining berries.

12. If the chocolate begins to cool and harden, simply reheat in the microwave in 30-second intervals, stirring in between each interval, to a temperature of between 85 and 90°F.

13. When the chocolate-covered berries have cooled completely and the chocolate has set, remove them to an airtight container and store in the refrigerator for up to 3 days.

SENSUAL SCAMPI

>> SERVES 4

The term *"aphrodisiac"* comes from the Greek goddess of love herself, Aphrodite. She was thought to be the epitome of desire and the goddess of love, sex, fertility, and beauty. Greek mythology states that she was born of the sea, which is why she is often depicted in the water or associated with seashells and was revered by seafarers. Because of her association with the sea, Aphrodite is a guardian of all things aquatic– therefore, all food from the ocean has aphrodisiac properties of love, lust, and romance.

You can make this dish with any seafood you like; scallops or lobster are wonderful additions or substitutions. However, if you are not able to eat shellfish, you can change the shrimp out for imitation crab or grilled whitefish like cod or haddock. This scampi features shrimp–be mindful of your intention as you sauté the shrimp in this dish. Notice the pink flesh of the shrimp and how delicate it is when you bite into it. Imbue the dish with sensual thoughts around the person with whom you might share this meal or the lover you intend to attract.

YOU WILL NEED:

Large pasta pot
1 pound dry linguine pasta
 (gluten-free also works well
 here)
Large skillet
2 tablespoons butter
1 tablespoon olive oil
3 garlic cloves, minced

1 pound raw shrimp, tail on,
 deveined
Juice of 2 lemons
¼ cup chopped fresh flat-leaf
 parsley
½ cup grated Pecorino Romano
 cheese, plus more for topping

1. Bring a large pot of water to a boil and cook pasta to package instructions.

2. Retain about ½ cup of starchy pasta water after draining the pasta and set aside.

3. While the water is boiling and pasta is cooking, prepare the scampi.

4. In a skillet over medium heat, warm the butter and oil until the butter is just melted.

5. Sauté the garlic in the butter and oil mixture until it becomes fragrant but not brown.

6. Add the shrimp, sautéing until they turn pink. Do not overcook or they will become rubbery.

7. Add half the lemon juice and reduce the heat.

8. Add the cooked linguine, the pasta water, and the remaining lemon juice.

9. Toss to coat, with the heat on medium-low, until the sauce reduces slightly, about 1 minute.

10. Turn the heat off and gently toss in the parsley and cheese to create a thicker sauce.

11. Serve immediately, topped with more cheese and parsley if desired.

AFFECTIONATE ASPARAGUS WITH HOLLANDAISE

>> SERVES 4

Foods that are known to have loving, lustful, or sensual energies often have shapes that are reminiscent of reproductive organs. These can be used for their innate magickal and energetic properties and can also be used symbolically due to their shape to encourage desire or arousal. Foods that suggest a phallic shape are typically used to symbolize masculine energies. When working with these energies, we must remember that there are celebrations of masculine energies within all of us. These foods are also associated with many masculine deities such as the Great Horned God, widely worshipped in Celtic and Germanic times; the Greek god Pan, the half-goat guardian of the wild and the hunt; and the Roman god Eros, god of desire and lust. All of these are associated with fertility, virility, and sex.

Asparagus has a long history of being associated with masculine energy, fertility, and virility. Its long stalks can be used in magickal cooking to increase lust and desire between consenting partners. It is important to note that these foods and energies can be worked with no matter your gender identity or sexual orientation. This recipe is designed to incite pleasurable experiences between sexual partners for whomever partakes in the dish. It includes a quick hollandaise sauce made from eggs and butter, where the eggs bring in another element of fertility magick.

Keep in mind that fertility magick does not always mean sexual. If you change your intention and visualization while making this recipe, you can focus on bringing fertile or creative energy and growth in non-sexual relationships as well as in physical ones. When you drizzle the sauce over the asparagus, envision covering your desires with energy that will make them grow and become reality.

YOU WILL NEED:

1 pound fresh asparagus
⅔ cup butter
Small saucepan
Heat-safe glass bowl

2 egg yolks
Whisk
Juice of 1 lemon
1 teaspoon white vinegar

1. Wash and cut off the bottom 1 inch of the asparagus stems so that there are no woody ends.

2. Dampen 2 paper towels, layer them, and wrap them around the asparagus, forming a bundle.

3. Microwave the asparagus bundle for 2 minutes. Remove from the microwave and unwrap from the paper towels. Use caution while removing the asparagus from the microwave, as it will be hot.

4. Lay the asparagus on a dry paper towel and set aside.

5. Melt the butter in the microwave in 30-second intervals, being sure to stir between each interval until fully melted. Do not boil or let it get foamy on top.

6. In the saucepan over medium-low heat, warm about 1 inch of water.

7. Place the glass bowl on top of the pan, making sure the water in the pot does not touch the bottom of the glass bowl.

8. Add the egg yolks to the bowl and whisk gently and consistently.

9. While continuing to whisk, slowly pour in the lemon juice and add the vinegar.

10. Continuing to whisk, drizzle in the butter, to slowly incorporate the fat of the butter with the egg yolks.

11. Whisk consistently until all the butter is incorporated and a light fluffy sauce forms.

12. Plate the prepared asparagus, drizzle the warm sauce over it, and serve immediately.

PART III

KITCHEN WITCHCRAFT FOR SPECIAL OCCASIONS

Kitchen witchcraft can be instrumental in creating small sacred moments of magick in your daily life but can also be honed for larger celebrations and more focused rituals. Broadening your practice beyond the daily routines of breakfast, lunch, and dinner to encompass specialized, focused workings may enrich your practice year-round and help create lasting traditions. For example, protection magick for the home, hearth, and family can become an altogether separate practice from the daily routine of making meals, through using specific protection foods and spell recipes. Likewise, deities and nature spirits may also be honored through the magick made in your kitchen by energetically inviting them into your space through your altar and offerings of food. Last, a large part of kitchen witchcraft is celebrating the seasons with feasts honoring the turning of the Wheel of the Year.

CHAPTER 9

PROTECTION OF THE HOME, HEART & SPIRITUAL SELF

From protecting the home with energetic boundaries to protecting the self with emotional boundaries, there are many ways in which kitchen witchcraft can aid in keeping your home, mind, and spirit safe. Focused protection magick may be done in the kitchen in small ways every day through mindfulness while whipping up snacks or during regular meal prep. However, it may be done quarterly in larger rituals or when you feel a particular need, like if there is a reason for concern about a specific issue or problem. By using foods that have innate energetic qualities of protection, warding, or foresight for protection magick, you may find the instances of bad or harmful things lessen in frequency and severity, which is the purpose of such work.

KNOT SPELL FOR WHOLE HOME PROTECTION

The kitchen is the beating heart of the home. And as such, the kitchen is where any hearth or family protection magick must start so that it is pumped through the rest of the home. There are many ways to incorporate protection magick from your kitchen throughout your home. One example is to line the outside of all doors and windows with salt to keep out any negative energies. Another is to keep garlic hung by your kitchen door to ward off any evil spirits from entering your kitchen, or so the folklore goes.

This Witches' Knot Spell, also known as a Witches' Ladder, is a practice that has been used for many centuries to focus energy into a cord. Since this spell is for protection of the whole home, it is suggested that this finished cord be hung at the main doorway to your home to ensure that any negative energy or unfriendly spirits cannot enter. Once the knots are tied, the energy of your focused visualization is stored in the cord, which can be hung anywhere within the home. If you have more than one entrance, repeat this process and make as many cords as needed. If possible, this spell should be renewed on each anniversary of the day you began living in the space. This spell can also be done in a shared space if you live with others, and then the cord can be placed at the entrance of any private space that is your own, to ward off unwanted energies in your personal space.

YOU WILL NEED:

Piece of paper
Pen

Piece of natural-fiber black cord, like cotton, preferably at least 1 yard in length and about ⅛ to ¼ inch thick

1. Sit in your kitchen space or the room in which food is prepared or shared.

2. Using your paper and pen, make a list of thirteen things, such as yourself, family, pets, home, and even your finances, that you would like to keep safe from harm, whether it is internal harm or from an external source.

3. Holding your cord at its full length, tie a knot on one end, as close to the end as possible. Then tie a knot at the other end, then the middle. With each knot you tie in the cord recite, out loud, one of the things from your list.

4. Tie a knot between the first side and the middle, then again between the second end, and the middle knot.

5. Continue in this pattern until you have thirteen knots in your cord, each one representing something or someone you wish to protect.

6. Hang your cord at the main entrance to your home or kitchen. Repeat this spell once a year and replace the previous year's cord to keep the spell potent.

MEDITATION FOR VISUALIZING
CALM BOUNDARIES

Protection of the emotional body, the space between the mental and physical body, is just as important as other forms of protection. Though this meditation can be done anywhere, it is best to keep it in the kitchen. By doing so, you keep the healthy and strong boundaries around yourself while you are in your most sacred of spaces and in sight of your focal point, your kitchen altar, which draws an energetic circle around any workings you do in this space. This meditation can be done in 10 or 20 minutes and repeated as often as needed.

YOU WILL NEED:

White candle and candleholder
Matches or a lighter
2 cups water

Large mug
Bag or sachet of your favorite herbal tea, nothing caffeinated

1. Place the candle on your kitchen altar and light it.

2. Pour the water into the mug and place it near the candle. Leave the tea bag near the cup but not in it, as you will use it later.

3. Dim the lights in the room to create a softer ambience if you like.

4. Find a comfortable seat in the kitchen where you can clearly see the candle burning. With your feet rooted, take three deep breaths in through the nose and out through the mouth. Actively relax your shoulders, jaw, and legs.

5. As you begin to relax and your breath starts to deepen, focus on the candle flame before you focus on the stillness of the water in the cup.

6. Close your eyes and continue to imagine the stillness of the water in the cup. Visualize this water as your emotions, calm and still.

7. Breathing deeply, imagine floating in water. In your mind's eye, imagine how it feels to be floating weightlessly in water. As this image and feeling of relaxation fill you up, visualize a large ring of trees surrounding you as you float. The trees are tall and thick.

8. Imagine feeling completely secure and safe behind this wall of trees as you float undisturbed in the warm water. In this meditative state, you are comfortable, unworried, and serene. The trees are protecting you from the outside world so that you can float effortlessly in the warm lake. Imagine now that your emotions are this lake, calm and undisturbed by the outside world. The trees are your boundaries, keeping out any harmful energies or thoughts that might disturb your calm state of being.

9. Once you feel the calm washing over you, pour the water into a kettle or pot and bring it to a boil. While waiting for the water to boil, continue to focus on feelings of peace and serenity enclosed in the pond surrounded by trees.

10. Once the water boils, pour it back into the mug to make your cup of tea.

11. Sip the tea. When you have finished the tea, extinguish the candle. Take with you the feeling of solace and comfort from the tree-shielded pond in your mind's eye.

FORETELLING LENTIL SOUP

≫ SERVES 4 TO 6

This hearty soup is not only comforting on a cold night but will also assist you in visualizing things to come, which can help you avoid harmful situations or choose different options to keep you safe and well. As you stir this soup clockwise, peer into the pot. As you watch the ingredients move around the pot with your stirring, visualize a question you want answered or situations you may want or need to avoid or move toward, and concentrate on the possible outcomes. Allow your mind to be open to whatever thoughts or images come in as messages while you are visualizing. The bay leaf in this recipe helps hone psychic abilities and open the third eye chakra, the intuition center of the spiritual self. Sage, when used in cooking, can affirm focus. In this soup, these herbs are brought together with the lentils, a powerful food for divination. By tapping into the power of the third eye and listening to your intuition to create foresight, it is possible to avoid mishaps or troubles, keeping you safe from harm or inconvenience.

YOU WILL NEED:

4 ounces dry brown lentils
Medium skillet
2 links sweet Italian pork sausage (optional)
Large sauce pot
2 tablespoons olive oil
1 large yellow onion, finely chopped
3 garlic cloves, minced
2 large carrots, chopped
2 celery stalks, chopped

8 cups organic low-sodium beef or vegetable broth
3 bay leaves, whole
2 tablespoons chopped fresh sage, or 1 teaspoon dried sage
2 tablespoons chopped fresh flat-leaf parsley
Salt
Freshly ground black pepper
8 ounces elbow macaroni or gluten-free elbow macaroni
Grated Parmesan cheese
Bread (optional)

1. Rinse the lentils in cold water and set aside.

2. Heat the skillet to medium-high heat. If you are including sausages, remove the meat from the casings and cook in the skillet until no pink remains, breaking up the meat so it has a crumbled texture. Remove from the heat and set aside.

3. In a large heavy-bottomed sauce pot over medium heat, warm the oil. Add the onion and garlic and cook, stirring consistently until the onion becomes translucent and the garlic is fragrant, about 3 minutes.

4. Add the carrots and celery and cook until they begin to soften slightly, about 3 minutes.

5. Add the broth, bay leaves, sage, parsley, lentils, and cooked sausage meat (if using).

6. Add salt and pepper to taste.

7. Turn the heat to low and simmer, stirring occasionally, about 45 minutes to an hour.

8. Meanwhile, about 30 minutes before the soup is ready, cook the macaroni according to package instructions, drain, and set aside.

9. When the soup is ready, fill individual serving bowls halfway with cooked macaroni. Fill the remainder of each bowl with soup.

10. Top with the cheese and fresh cracked pepper if desired.

11. Serve immediately with a side of hearty bread for dipping (if using). Be sure to remove the bay leaves before serving; they should not be consumed.

KEEP SAFE GARLIC BREAD

≫ MAKES 1 LOAF

Garlic is revered as a food for protection magick. As far back as ancient Egypt, garlic was thought to ward off illness and increase endurance. In the time of the Roman Empire, garlic was thought to give strength and courage to its army and so was given to soldiers. For centuries, European folklore has heralded the protective powers of garlic for warding off evil and illnesses brought on by evil. These ideas may have come from garlic's natural antibiotic properties and ability to boost the immune system. For these reasons, kitchen witches have been using garlic in protection magick for years.

Garlic is a multiuse ingredient that can flavor everything from eggs to breads, sauces, and salad dressings. It can be dried, roasted, pureed, sautéed, and pickled. Magickally speaking, adding garlic to any dish can incorporate protective energies into your dishes. For example, adding garlic to a tomato sauce wraps a layer of protection energy around the love energy of the tomatoes. If you are gluten sensitive, skip the dough-making part of this recipe and simply make the garlic butter to drizzle on top of gluten-free bread.

YOU WILL NEED:

1 packet active dry yeast, about 2 teaspoons
¾ cup warm water
2¾ cups all-purpose flour
1 teaspoon salt
1 tablespoon olive oil, plus 3 tablespoons
3 tablespoons butter
6 garlic cloves, minced
¼ cup chopped fresh parsley

1. In a small bowl, combine the yeast and warm water. Stir gently and let rest 5 to 10 minutes until the yeast blooms and small bubbles or foam appear.

2. In a large bowl, combine the flour and salt.

3. Add 1 tablespoon of the olive oil and the yeast mixture to the flour. Stir until sticky.

4. On a lightly greased surface, begin to knead the dough until it is smooth and elastic.

5. Place in a lightly greased bowl and cover with plastic wrap and a dish cloth. Set aside in a warm spot on the counter for about 60 to 90 minutes until the dough has doubled in size.

6. Using your fist, gently push down into the center of the dough to deflate it. Turn it into a ball and cover again for about 30 minutes.

7. Cut the dough into three even portions and roll each out into a long rope shape, about 18 inches long and about 1½ inches thick.

8. On a lightly greased baking sheet, braid the ropes and tuck the ends underneath.

9. Cover the braided loaf with a kitchen towel and let rest another 60 minutes.

10. When the 60 minutes is almost up, heat the oven to 425°F.

11. In a small saucepan, melt the butter.

12. Add the garlic, the remaining 3 tablespoons of olive oil, and the parsley, and stir until the garlic begins to sizzle

13. Remove from the heat. Using a pastry brush, gently brush about 1 or 2 tablespoons of the garlic butter mixture on top of the loaf. Reserve the rest for later.

14. Bake the loaf for 30 minutes. Remove from the oven and let cool for about 15 minutes.

15. Brush or drizzle the remaining garlic butter over the top of the loaf or serve it alongside for drizzling on cut slices.

SANCTUARY SKIRT STEAK WITH HORSERADISH SAUCE

>> SERVES 4

Horseradish root is thought to have protective energies due to its strong flavor and association with fire energies. The link to fire energy comes from the burning or tingling to the sinuses that occurs when eating this root vegetable. The horseradish sauce in this recipe can be doubled and refrigerated for use in other dishes, like on sandwiches or fish. This recipe calls for fresh grated horseradish, but you can use jarred if you cannot find fresh. Since beef holds the energy of prosperity, while spooning this horseradish sauce on top of your steak, envision covering your home, assets, and career in a blanket of protection. If you do not eat meat, you can replace the steak in this recipe with large grilled portobello mushrooms and just use the same rub on them before grilling.

YOU WILL NEED:

1 teaspoon salt
1 teaspoon granulated onion
1 teaspoon granulated garlic
1 teaspoon paprika
1 teaspoon sugar
1 teaspoon freshly ground black pepper
2 tablespoons olive oil
2 pounds skirt steak
Grill or grill pan for a stove
Cooking spray

FOR THE SAUCE:

1 cup sour cream
¼ cup fresh grated horseradish or jarred horseradish
1 tablespoon mayonnaise
1 tablespoon mustard
1 tablespoon chopped scallion
Salt
Freshly ground black pepper

1. In a medium bowl, combine the salt, granulated onion, granulated garlic, paprika, sugar, pepper, and oil. Mix well to form a paste rub for the steak.

2. Generously coat the steak with the rub and set aside, covered, at room temperature for at least 30 minutes.

3. Heat the grill or grill pan on the stove to medium-high heat.

4. Spray the surface with cooking spray and grill the meat to the desired temperature.

5. While the meat is cooking, make the sauce by mixing the sour cream, horseradish, mayonnaise, mustard, scallion, and salt and pepper to taste in a bowl until well combined.

6. When the steak is done cooking, remove it from the heat and let it rest before slicing.

7. Serve the steak topped with the horseradish sauce. Store the remaining sauce in an airtight container in the refrigerator for up to 2 weeks.

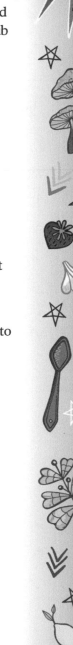

CHAPTER 10

WORSHIPPING DEITIES & SPIRITUAL GUIDES

It's up to each individual practitioner to determine what role deities or spiritual guides should play in their life and their home. Some kitchen witches find connection with deities specific to that space, like Brigid the Celtic goddess of the hearth or Zao Jun the god of the kitchen and home in Chinese folklore. But an entity does not need to have specific dominion over the kitchen or home to be part of your practice. Nor are you obligated to invite anyone not aligned with your beliefs and values.

Like friends at a party, you choose the guest list and how to make them comfortable. If you choose to work in collaboration with gods, guides, nature, spirits, or your ancestors, it is important that you welcome them into your home as you would a friend, showing them respect and hospitality. In this chapter, you will learn spells, rituals, and recipes to create space or make offerings. Each one is intended as a framework, with room left open for you to personalize it.

INVITING THE GODS AND
SPIRITS TO YOUR TABLE

Calling in or welcoming deities, spirits, or ancestors into your kitchen space is a wonderful way to unite these energies with your magickal workings. This particular calling ritual is designed to be performed no matter which energy you'd like to accompany you in the kitchen. It's most effective when used for a specific celebration, meal, gathering, or spell working, rather than as an open invitation to your daily life.

YOU WILL NEED:

Bell or chime for vibrational energy clearing

Matches or a lighter

White candle and candleholder, to represent the sun

Black candle and candleholder, to represent the moon

Small bowl salt, to represent earth

Incense, to represent air

Small red candle, to represent fire

Small bowl water, to represent water

Talisman, such as a sacred object, photo, or trinket, to symbolize the spirit or deity you are calling in; for example, a photo of a relative who has passed on, a statue or illustration of a deity like the goddess Brigid, or an acorn or bell to welcome faeries

1. Stand in front of your altar in your kitchen facing north.

2. Starting in this direction, use your bell or chimes to clear the energy, ringing it once or twice in the direction of the north, moving clockwise to the west, then to the south, and then to the east.

3. Light the white candle and say: *I call on the power of the sun, the God, the masculine, the keeper of the light. I welcome you.*

4. Light the black candle and say: *I call on the power of the moon, the Goddess, the feminine, the keeper of the night. I welcome you.*

5. Holding the bowl of salt, say: *I call on the power of the earth, steadfast and life-giving. I welcome you.*

6. Holding the incense in its holder (if it is a stick of incense, you may hold it by the end) light it. Once the stream of smoke begins, say: *I call on the power of the air, inspiring and adaptable. I welcome you.*

7. Holding the red candle, light it and say: *I call on the power of fire, transformative and powerful. I welcome you.*

8. Holding the bowl of water in your hands, say: *I call on the power of water, compassionate and wise. I welcome you.*

9. Holding the talisman, invite the energy of your chosen deity or spirit into your kitchen. Say three times:

   I call upon you, _____
   With joy and comfort my table surround
   So, magickal meals and love abound
   Hail and welcome!

10. When you have finished, place the symbol or photo in a prominent place on your altar and continue with any meals or work you need to do. When the meal, chore, or gathering is over, stand in front of the altar as you did before.

11. Hold the talisman again, and this time say:

    I thank and release you, _____
    Stay if you will, go if you must
    Hail and farewell

12. You can repeat this ritual anytime to invite any spirits or deities into the kitchen. Be sure to do the releasing when your work, meal, or gathering is over.

CHARMING CHARM BAGS

You can always bring the magick of your kitchen with you in the form of a charm bag or sachet. This is a portable spell in a pouch, created from common kitchen items. While they can be stored on your kitchen altar, they can also be worn or carried with you throughout the day.

A particularly versatile form of magick, charm bags can be used to honor a chosen deity or spirit. In this case, you'll need to put thought, care, and research into choosing ingredients that coincide with the energy of the being you'd like to call on. But how you incorporate those elements is entirely up to your instinct. For example, to bring Aphrodite, the goddess of love, into your kitchen workings, you might choose a pink bag, rose quartz and dried rose petals for love, hot pepper flakes for passion, a small heart charm, and a piece of paper with a love-related intention written on it. The glorious goodness of these bags is that you can make them in honor of any deity or spirit you want. Following is a list of common elements and correspondences to help you start thinking about your own charm bag. There are endless combinations of your creative charm-making here.

YOU WILL NEED:

Small bag with a drawstring closure

Bag colors: Black for moon or lunar goddesses; white for sun or solar gods; green for faeries or nature spirits; brown or tan for animal spirits; red or pink for love, passion, or romance deities; blue or purple for wisdom or knowledge deities

Suggested stones or crystals for love: rose quartz, garnet, opal, quartz

Suggested stones or crystals for prosperity: agate, jade, jasper, topaz

Suggested stones or crystals for grounding: onyx, tiger's eye, hematite

Suggested stones or crystals for peace: turquoise, amethyst, tanzanite

Herbs to honor hearth and home deities: cinnamon, basil, nutmeg, milk thistle, rosemary

Suggested additions: jewelry charms like hearts, stars, pentacles, or moons for honoring deities. Trinkets like bells, acorns, dried mushrooms, and shiny coins for honoring faeries or nature spirits. Written phases, poetry, or intentions in celebration or in honor of the chosen entity.

FAERIE RING TOADSTOOL SOUP (MUSHROOM SOUP)

>> MAKES ABOUT 6-8 SERVINGS

Faeries or nature spirits are known to be creative, organized, and cooperative to a kitchen witch's workings, but inviting them to join you in the kitchen can be tricky. Though many arrive with the intention to help, especially in the kitchen, some are mischievous and could sneak in alongside well-mannered ones. Cooking a meal made with ingredients that are symbolic of the faerie realm is one way to open your space for them to join you. Ingredients such as nuts, honey, fruit, and candy are perfect for attracting these energies. But the ingredient most popularly associated with the faeries is the mushroom. Legend has it that rings of mushrooms or toadstools that pop up seemingly overnight are portals to the faerie realm. The Fae, as they are sometime called, encompass many different energies and entities associated with the world of nature and woodland magick. So leave a thimbleful of this soup near a faerie door—or outside near a wooded area—to let your faerie friends know they are appreciated and that you desire their magick to touch your life, home, and cooking.

YOU WILL NEED:

Large (5-quart) sauce pot
2 tablespoons butter
2 tablespoons olive oil
16 ounces sliced button
   mushrooms
1 medium yellow onion, sliced
3 cloves garlic, chopped
2 tablespoons cornstarch
½ cup white wine (optional)

5 cups low-sodium chicken broth
   or vegetable broth
1 large russet potato, peeled and
   cut into cubes
1 tablespoon fresh thyme, plus
   more for topping
Blender
½ cup heavy (whipping) cream
Salt
Freshly ground black pepper

1. In a large sauce pot over medium heat, warm the butter and oil. Add the mushrooms and onion.

2. Cook the mushrooms and onion on medium heat for about 10 to 15 minutes or until the mushrooms start to brown slightly. They will reduce in size and soften.

3. Add the garlic and sauté another 2 minutes until the garlic starts to soften.

4. Add the cornstarch and continue stirring to coat everything well.

5. Add the wine (if using), stirring until it has reduced by about a quarter.

6. Add the broth, potato, and thyme. Cover and reduce heat.

7. Let simmer on low heat for 30 minutes.

8. Working in batches, gently ladle the soup into a blender. Leave about 3 inches of room at the top of the blender and do not seal the lid completely or the steam from the hot liquid may make the top of the blender pop off. Puree the soup and put it back in a pot on the stove.

9. When all the soup is pureed and returned to low heat on the stove, add the cream and stir gently to incorporate.

10. Add salt and pepper to taste and serve immediately topped with fresh thyme.

MOON MOTHER RAVIOLI

⟫ MAKES 4-6 SERVINGS

One of the most popular feminine deities worshipped by witches is the Triple Goddess, also referred to as the Goddess and represented by the moon in all phases—waxing, full, and waning. In ancient Celtic and Druidic times, these associations were made to represent the cycles of a woman's life. The phases being maiden or the time before adolescence, mother or the time of adulthood or child rearing, and crone or when all children have grown. Although the word "crone" can have a negative connotation, among witches, crones are celebrated as elders in the community and are often responsible for handing down traditions. In spring, the earth is in her maiden phase, filled with promise and renewal. In summer, she is the mother, full of abundance. In fall and winter, she is the crone, restful and introspective while the earth is sleeping.

No matter what your gender identity, all human beings, like the earth, go through cycles of growth. Consider calling upon the Goddess's different aspects at various times of the year in the cycle of your life. The following recipe focuses on using food as symbolic magick, using cheese-filled ravioli as symbols for the full moon, filled with joyful energy and dressed with a creamy Alfredo sauce.

YOU WILL NEED:

Large (5-quart) sauce pot
Salt
Large skillet
½ cup butter
3 garlic cloves, minced
2 cups heavy (whipping) cream
2 tablespoons cornstarch
1 ounce cream cheese

½ teaspoon dried oregano
½ teaspoon dried parsley
Freshly ground black pepper
Pinch nutmeg
2 pounds fresh cheese ravioli, round not square
1 cup grated Pecorino Romano cheese

1. Fill the sauce pot with water and a pinch of salt. Set on the stove but do not turn the heat on.

2. In a large skillet over medium heat, melt the butter.

3. Add the garlic and sauté until fragrant and just soft. Do not overcook.

4. Add the heavy cream, cornstarch, and cream cheese, stirring on medium-low heat until the cream cheese has melted fully.

5. Turn the heat on under the pot of water and bring to a boil.

6. As the water is coming to a boil, continue to whisk your cheese sauce mixture, adding the oregano, parsley, salt, pepper, and nutmeg to taste.

7. When the water has boiled, add the ravioli and cook them until they float to the surface.

8. While the ravioli are cooking, whisk the cheese into your sauce. Simmer for about 3 minutes, stirring frequently to ensure the sauce does not burn.

9. When the ravioli are cooked, drain and plate immediately. Spoon the cheese sauce over the ravioli and top with fresh chopped parsley, pepper to taste, and more cheese if desired.

CERNUNNOS CARROT CAKE

>> MAKES 1 CAKE

Regardless of personal gender identity, all humans hold energies of masculine and feminine, sun and moon. It is up to you when and how these energies are expressed. A popular masculine deity for witches is the Horned God, who wears many faces, such as the Hern, Green Man, Oak King, and Cernunnos. He is associated with the sun, life, animals, and fertility in all forms. Common fertility magick is not just about pro-creation, but about bringing new life to ideas, situations, and creative endeavors.

This recipe uses carrots as a symbol of the Horned God's fertility powers. Combining the energy of the carrots in this recipe with the spices of cinnamon, nutmeg, ginger, and clove enhances the sun energy in the cake.

YOU WILL NEED:

9 x 13-inch baking dish, 2 or 3 inches deep
Parchment paper
Cooking spray or butter for greasing the pan
2 large bowls
2½ cups all-purpose flour or gluten-free all-purpose flour
1½ teaspoons baking powder
1½ teaspoons baking soda
½ teaspoon kosher salt
1 tablespoon ground cinnamon
1 teaspoon ground ginger
½ teaspoon ground nutmeg
½ teaspoon ground cloves
Electric mixer
2 cups packed dark brown sugar
1 cup vegetable oil
4 eggs
¾ cup crushed pineapple
1 teaspoon vanilla extract
2 cups grated carrots
1 cup chopped walnuts (optional)

FOR THE FROSTING

8 ounces cream cheese, softened
¼ cup unsalted butter, softened
2 cups powdered sugar
½ teaspoon vanilla extract

1. Preheat the oven to 350°F.

2. Line the baking dish with parchment paper, cutting it to fit the pan and go up the sides evenly. Spray or grease the parchment paper in the pan and set aside.

3. In a large bowl, combine the flour, baking powder, baking soda, salt, and all the spices. Whisk or sift well.

4. In a large bowl, using an electric mixer on low speed, mix the brown sugar, oil, eggs, pineapple, and vanilla until there are no lumps remaining.

5. Gently stir the dry ingredients into the wet ingredients.

6. Fold in the grated carrots and walnuts (if using).

7. Spoon the batter into the prepared pan and smooth out with a spatula if necessary. The batter will be thick.

8. Bake for 45 to 55 minutes until a cake tester comes out clean and the top is just golden.

9. Set on a wire rack to cool completely before removing from the pan.

10. Make the frosting by combining all the frosting ingredients in a medium bowl and blending with an electric mixer on high speed for about 3 minutes, until smooth and creamy.

11. When the cake is completely cooled, remove from the pan and discard the parchment paper.

12. Spread a thin layer of frosting on the cake and serve at room temperature or chilled overnight. Store leftover cake in an airtight container in the refrigerator up to a week.

CHAPTER 11

HONORING SEASONAL DAYS OR THE LESSER SABBATS

One of the cornerstones of kitchen witchcraft is celebrating the turning of the Wheel of the Year. This is a calendar of sorts that modern witches use to mark the seasonal changes of the year. There are four major holidays, or Sabbats, marked by the solstices and equinoxes, and four lesser holidays or Lesser Sabbats, marked by the halfway points between them. For example, the celebration of Beltane falls on May 1 and is the halfway point between the spring equinox, around March 21, and the summer solstice, which falls around June 22. The Lesser Sabbats are not really considered "less" to most witches. In fact, they are some of the most important days on the Wheel of the Year. They include Imbolc, Beltane, Lammas, and Samhain. In this chapter, you will learn to celebrate the Wheel with drinks, feasts, and festivities to mark the year by bringing people together or celebrating quietly.

SEASONAL HERBAL INCENSE

Celebrating the turning of the Wheel of the Year with small acknowledgments keeps you in communion with the changing seasons. A simple ritual that can be done anytime is burning incense. This practice is made even more special if the herbal incense blend is one made with your intention for honoring the seasons. If you do not have one already, keep a Wheel of the Year somewhere close to your altar and turn it as the seasons change. Your wheel can be store-bought, homemade, or simply printed out from an image online. When the date is appropriate, rotate the appropriate holiday to the top of the wheel. Each time you turn your wheel, burn the incense blend associated with the season to honor the change.

The incense blends for each season listed here can be burned in small amounts or can be tossed by the handful into ritual bonfires for enhanced magick at larger rituals. But they should always be designed and measured in equal parts. For example, if you use 2 tablespoons of pine needles, you should include 2 tablespoons of both cedar and frankincense. Any remaining dried herbal incense can be stored for up to a year in airtight containers.

YOU WILL NEED:

Mortar and pestle

For winter incense, to welcome good fortune in the year to come: equal parts dried pine needles, cedar, and frankincense

For spring incense, to renew the soul and celebrate the rebirth of the earth: equal parts dried lavender, rosemary, and lemongrass

For summer incense, to embrace the fullness of the season in all its abundance: equal parts dried rose, sweetgrass, and sunflower petals

For autumn incense, to warm the heart for the cold months to come: equal parts dried sage, cinnamon bark (preferably in small chips), and mugwort

≫ **A note on burning the ingredients:** Be sure your herbs are fully dried and do not contain any moisture. Always burn incense in a heat-resistant container like a cast-iron burner or abalone shell.

1. Gather the ingredients for the herbal incense blend you are planning to make.

2. Put a small amount of each herb into the mortar. Using the pestle, grind the herbs together in sets of three repetitions. Recite this incantation with each movement of the pestle:

   The Wheel of the Year draws the season near
   With these herbs I'll burn to celebrate its turn

3. When you have finished grinding all the herbs in the batch you want to make, put it in an airtight container labeled for the season you will burn it.

4. When ready to use, burn your herb incense in a safe place as desired.

IMBOLC (FEBRUARY 1)—EARTH'S FIRE RED PEPPER SAUCE

>> SERVES 4

Imbolc is the first of the Lesser Sabbats on the Wheel. It comes on February 1 at the halfway point between the winter solstice and the spring equinox. The word "Imbolc" comes from the ancient Celtic or Gaelic word meaning ewe's milk. For the Celts, this was the time of year when the ewes began to get pregnant and make milk for their soon-to-be-born babies. This signaled the warming of the earth and the coming of spring. Over the centuries, Imbolc, or February 1, has been associated with the goddess Brigid, the goddess of fire, hearth, and home.

When celebrating Imbolc, connecting with sun or fire energy is appropriate as the celebration energetically encourages the warmth held in the earth, even when the weather is still cold. Foods like peppers—be they spicy or mild—are a direct correlation to the fire energy of Imbolc. Other Imbolc foods can include spices like ginger, turmeric, and curry. Using red bell peppers and crushed chili flakes in this Imbolc recipe, focus on the warming of the earth as you stir the sauce. The recommended pasta for this sauce is rotelle, or wagon wheel pasta, to symbolize the Wheel of the Year, but you can use any pasta you prefer, including gluten-free pasta. As you cook this meal, envision the center of the earth's core—warm, full of life, and radiating heat to the surface—chasing away the last hold of winter's chill.

YOU WILL NEED:

Large (5-quart) sauce pot
2 tablespoons olive oil
2 large red bell peppers, chopped
1 white onion, chopped
3 garlic cloves, minced

2 (15-ounce) cans crushed tomatoes
1 tablespoon dried basil
1 tablespoon granulated garlic
¼ cup red wine
Salt

Freshly ground black pepper
1 teaspoon crushed red pepper or chili flakes (optional)
16 ounces dry pasta of your choice

¼ cup shaved Asiago cheese for garnish (optional)
1 tablespoon chopped fresh flat-leaf parsley

1. In a large sauce pot over medium heat, warm the oil.

2. Add the bell peppers and onions, sautéing until both start to become tender.

3. Add the minced garlic and cook an additional 2 or 3 minutes until the garlic begins to soften.

4. Add the tomatoes, basil, granulated garlic, wine, and salt and pepper to taste, stirring well to combine.

5. Stir in the crushed red pepper (if using), using less or more for your desired heat level.

6. Lower the heat and let the sauce simmer for at least 2 hours, stirring every 30 minutes.

7. Thirty minutes before serving, cook the pasta according to package instructions.

8. When the pasta is cooked and drained, plate it immediately and ladle the sauce on top.

9. Sprinkle with the Asiago cheese (if using), parsley, and more chili flakes (if using).

BELTANE (MAY 1)—MAY DAY LAVENDER LEMONADE

⟫ MAKES 72 OUNCES

Beltane is one of the most widely celebrated holidays of the year for the witchcraft and Pagan communities. It is a celebration of the return of the sun, when spring is in full swing, flowers are blooming, bees are buzzing, and life is blossoming all around. On the Wheel of the Year, Beltane falls at the halfway point between the spring equinox and the summer solstice. It is also the exact opposite on the Wheel from Samhain. It is said that, at the time of Beltane, the veil between our world and the world of the faeries and nature spirits is the thinnest. As such, this is an optimal time to work with those energies should you choose to do so, with offerings of sweet fruits, cakes, shiny objects, or flowers.

Beltane is traditionally celebrated outdoors with maypole dances, music, merriment, and, of course, lots and lots of food. Picnics, cookouts, and bonfires that last into the night are often where witches can be found on this holiday. Beltane foods range from sweet to savory and are mostly those that are in season. Fresh herbs, eggs, berries, spring green salads, sweet cakes, and drinks kissed with honey and lemon are all appropriate for Beltane.

No springtide celebration would be complete without cool refreshments. This Lavender Lemonade is a perfect pairing for your Beltane celebrations and can be adorned with fresh blueberries or spiked with a little vodka if you choose to celebrate in this way. You may want to make extra because this perfectly purple drink tends to be a crowd-pleaser.

YOU WILL NEED:

Medium (3-quart) sauce pot
Pitcher, 72- to 80-ounce capacity

4 cups water and 3 cups cold water, divided

2 cups sugar
4 lavender herbal tea bags
1¾ cups freshly squeezed lemon
  juice
Lemon slices, for serving
  (optional)

Blueberries, for serving
  (optional)
Lavender sprigs, for serving
  (optional)

1. In a medium sauce pot, bring 4 cups of water and the sugar to a boil.

2. Stir until all the sugar has dissolved and bring back to a soft boil.

3. Turn the heat off and add the lavender tea bags to the hot water.

4. Let the tea steep for 3 to 5 minutes.

5. Remove the lavender tea bags and let cool until room temperature, about an hour.

6. In a large pitcher, combine the 3 cups cold water, the lemon juice, and the cooled lavender tea.

7. Stir well and chill until ready to serve.

8. Pour into glasses over ice and garnish with lemon slices, blueberries, or lavender sprigs (if using).

LAMMAS (AUGUST 1)— LIFE OF THE LAND CORN BREAD

≫ SERVES 8

The holiday of Lammas, also called Lughnasadh, marks the halfway point between the summer solstice and the autumn equinox. It is the first of the three harvest festivals on the Wheel of the Year. *Lammas* translates to Loaf Mass, denoting the importance of bread being made at this time to mark the start of the grain harvest.

Today, this holiday is celebrated by witches and pagans with feasts of bread and seasonal foods. There is an element of gratitude that permeates celebrations for Lammas. Feast foods include grains like corn, wheat, barley, and rye. They also include an abundance of summer squashes, tomatoes, fresh herbs, lettuce, fish, and stone fruits.

This corn bread recipe is gluten-free and is perfect to accompany any of your Lammas celebrations, as corn represents the cycles of the growing season. As you enjoy this bread, give thanks to the earth for all she gives throughout the year. Although the recipe here calls for a cast-iron skillet, you can make this in a well-greased round 10-inch baking pan—simply skip step 2 and step 7.

YOU WILL NEED:

- 10-inch oven-safe skillet, preferably cast-iron
- 1½ cups gluten-free all-purpose flour
- ½ cup corn flour
- 1¼ cups fine cornmeal
- 4 teaspoons baking powder
- ½ teaspoon salt
- Stand mixer with a whisk attachment, or a large mixing bowl and handheld electric mixer
- ⅔ cup butter, softened, plus 1 tablespoon butter
- ½ cup sugar
- 3 eggs
- 1⅔ cups milk

1. Preheat the oven to 400°F.

2. Put the cast-iron pan in the oven to preheat the pan.

3. In a medium bowl, combine the flour, corn flour, cornmeal, baking powder, and salt. Set aside.

4. In the bowl of the stand mixer, cream together the ⅔ cup softened butter, the sugar, and the eggs on medium-low speed.

5. Slowly mix in the milk, pouring gently as the mixer continues at medium-low speed, until well combined.

6. Add the flour mixture one cup at a time, mixing on low until the flour is just combined. Do not overmix.

7. Remove the hot skillet from the oven and coat generously with the remaining 1 tablespoon of butter. The pan will be very hot, so be careful when working with it. The butter should melt easily and quickly in the hot pan, but be sure to coat the pan evenly.

8. Add the batter to the pan and bake for 30 to 40 minutes until the top is golden brown and a tester comes out clean.

9. Let the bread cool on a wire rack for 20 minutes. Serve warm with a drizzle of honey if desired.

10. Store in an airtight container for up to a week.

SAMHAIN (OCTOBER 31)– HONORING THE ANCESTORS APPLE GLAZED PORK CHOPS

≫ SERVES 4

Samhain falls on October 31 and is considered the witch's new year. Signaling the end of the year, the last harvest, and the start of winter, Samhain is an important holiday for witches. Samhain shares its date with Halloween, All Souls' Night, and the eve of the Day of the Dead. It is thought that the veil between our world and the world of the dead is the thinnest at Samhain. Meals for the beloved dead, setting a place at the table, or offerings of wine on Samhain night are wonderful ways to honor and welcome those who have passed.

This flavorful stuffed pork chop is a contemporary meal that harkens back to celebrations of ancient times where meats, roasted birds, and spiced apples were the stars. A sweet glaze made from apple jelly and maple syrup and drizzled over this tender stuffed chop makes a memorable meal to honor the season and those who have left this world. For a meatless option, use this stuffing inside a roasted butternut squash.

YOU WILL NEED:

2 pork rib chops
Large oven-safe skillet
3 tablespoons olive oil, divided
½ white onion, chopped
2 celery stalks, finely chopped
1 tablespoon chopped fresh sage
1 tablespoon chopped fresh rosemary
2 cups toasted breadcrumbs or unflavored stuffing mix, or gluten-free stuffing mix

2 Granny Smith apples, peeled and chopped into ¼-inch pieces
¼ cup golden raisins
1 cup chicken stock
Salt
Freshly ground black pepper
1 cup apple jelly
1 tablespoon maple syrup
2 tablespoons apple cider

1. Preheat the oven to 350°F.

2. Using a sharp knife, cut the pork chops along the side, creating a pocket.

3. In the skillet over medium-high heat, warm 2 tablespoons of the oil.

4. Add the onions, celery, sage, and rosemary to the skillet and sauté until onions are tender and translucent. Do not brown. Add salt and pepper to taste.

5. Add the breadcrumbs, apples, golden raisins, and chicken stock and remove from the heat.

6. Using a spoon, scoop the stuffing into the pockets of the pork chops but do not overfill. Set the stuffed chops on a plate and transfer any remaining stuffing to an oven-safe dish.

7. Wipe down the skillet with a warm cloth to remove any bits left over from the stuffing.

8. Heat the remaining 1 tablespoon of olive oil in the skillet over medium heat.

9. Cook the pork chops about 3 minutes on each side until the edges are starting to brown.

10. Leaving the pork in the skillet, bake in the oven for 35 minutes until cooked through.

11. While the pork is cooking, create the glaze.

12. In a small sauce pot, heat the apple jelly, maple syrup, and apple cider, stirring until the jelly has melted down and the consistency is smooth.

13. When the pork chops are done, spoon the sauce over them and serve immediately.

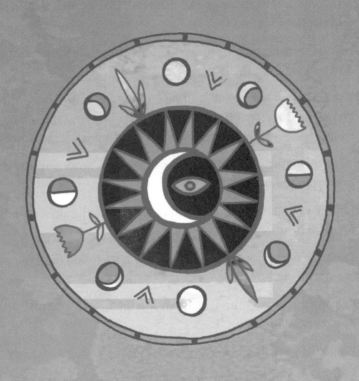

CHAPTER 12

CELEBRATING SOLAR HOLIDAYS & FESTIVALS

This chapter dives a bit deeper into how to celebrate the higher holidays, or Sabbats. These are also known as the solar festivals, having to do with the position of the sun in the sky at certain times of year. These Sabbats chart the quarters of the year: Yule at the winter solstice, Ostara at the spring equinox, Litha at the summer solstice, and Mabon at the autumn equinox. These are times of the year where a kitchen witch really shines—setting a magickal table, cooking a delicious meal, and gathering loved ones to celebrate each season as the Wheel of the Year turns. Setting your magickal table seasonally is one tradition that may enhance all the celebratory feasts you will create in your magickal kitchen. As you explore cooking for the Sabbats in this chapter, get inspired with ideas for feasts, gatherings, and even gift-giving.

MAGICKAL TABLE CENTERPIECES
FOR FESTIVE FEASTS

Each season brings a unique feeling and energy of its own to the home and the kitchen. By creating a seasonal table, you and your guests may feel more connected to the meal, and the energy, conversation, and merriment between you can flow more freely.

Each one of the following centerpieces can be used for the entire season for which it is named. Dishes, drinks, and meals can be enjoyed around this centerpiece for all the Sabbats on the Wheel of the Year that fit into the appropriate season. Choose your items mindfully and intentionally. When setting them out, thank them for their presence at your table in the months to come. When putting them away for the season, hold each one of the objects and thank it for holding the memories made around it. If you have any perishable objects, thank them and dispose of them.

≫ WINTER ≫

YOU WILL NEED:

Toothpick
4 large oranges
Jar cloves

Large wooden bowl
Pine boughs

1. Using the toothpick, gently poke holes in the oranges in decorative designs.

2. Stick a clove in each hole. Place the cloved oranges in the bowl and decorate with the pine boughs.

3. Place the bowl in the center of the table and enjoy the festive smell and sight at each meal.

⫸ SPRING ⫸

YOU WILL NEED

2 pillar candleholders
2 pillar candles in pink for love
    and renewal
Narrow tray or plate about
    12 inches long by 5 or 6 inches
    wide

Dried flowers such as roses,
    lavender, pansies, forsythia, or
    violets

1. Place the candles in their candleholders equidistant from the center of the tray.

2. Fill the tray with the seasonal dried flowers.

3. Light the pink candles during meals and gatherings.

⫸ SUMMER ⫸

YOU WILL NEED

Bright yellow or orange cloth
    about 6 inches by 6 inches
5 sunflowers (real or fake) to
    represent five elements: earth,
    air, fire, water, spirit

Large clear vase
4 pieces of carnelian crystal, to
    represent the fire and warmth
    of the sun

1. Place the cloth in the center of the table.

2. Trim each sunflower stem to comfortably fit the vase and fill the vase with water. If you are using real sunflowers, you will need to replace them weekly.

3. Place the vase on the cloth.

CONTINUED ⫸

4. Place each piece of carnelian around the base of the vase in each direction, starting with the north, then the east, then the west, and finally the south.

5. Gather around this summer table decoration and celebrate the brilliance of the season.

≫ AUTUMN ≫

YOU WILL NEED

Table runner or piece of fabric in orange, brown, or tan, about 12 to 18 inches long and 6 inches wide

4 glass votive candleholders and votive candles

4 glass lanterns of different shapes and sizes appropriate to the size of your table

Bag mixed nuts with the shells on

8 branches dried oak leaves

1. Lay the fabric or table runner in the center of your table.

2. Place a votive with candle inside each of the lanterns.

3. Surround the votive with nuts and close the lantern to contain the nuts.

4. Place the lanterns side by side on the table runner and lay the oak branches around the lanterns.

5. Light the candles for gathering or dinners through the season.

6. At the end of the season, empty the lanterns of the nuts and place them outdoors, offering them to animals and nature as the cold winter months loom.

YULE, THE WINTER SOLSTICE (DECEMBER 21 TO 23)— TRADITIONAL WINTER WASSAIL

◇◇

>> SERVES 12

Yule has been celebrated at the winter solstice for centuries. The longest night of the year, when the daylight hours are the shortest, this event celebrates the beginning of the end of long nights. It is a celebration of the rebirth of the sun because each day after the solstice the sun gets stronger and brighter. In Norse tradition, the holiday is known as Jul, where All-Father Odin rides his eight-legged horse through the night sky. In Roman times, this solstice was celebrated with feasts and dancing as Saturnalia, the celebration of Saturn, the god of time and farming. Celtic and Druidic peoples celebrated the season with boughs of evergreens and pine trees in their homes, to give the nature spirits a place to rest in the bitter winter months.

A popular holiday song chimes "here we come a caroling among the leaves so green," but in this folk song's origins, dating back hundreds of years, the lyric was "a-wassailing." The word "wassail" translates to "to your health," a traditional saying when raising a glass in toasting at special occasions. To go "a-wassailing" in ages past meant you would literally walk around villages and neighborhoods raising a glass to the health of their kin and townsfolk. Over the years, the tradition of wintertide well-wishing has become synonymous with caroling instead of drinking libations. Because this toast was done with a warm spiced cider, the drink became named for the act. This recipe is best made in a slow cooker for at least four hours and can be a warm welcome to guests as they arrive for any Yuletide celebrations. If you choose to imbibe this libation outdoors while wishing your neighbors happy holidays, be sure to offer some to the nature spirits among the evergreens on winter solstice night.

YOU WILL NEED:

Large (5- or 6-quart)
  slow cooker
1½ gallons fresh apple cider
1 large orange
1 large apple
4 cinnamon sticks, plus more for
  serving (optional)

2 whole nutmegs
1 tablespoon whole allspice
3 anise stars (optional)
¼ cup honey
2 cups brandy or rum

1. Set the slow cooker on the low setting.

2. Pour in the apple cider.

3. Slice the orange and the apple in half horizontally, revealing the five-pointed star inside the apple and the sunlike burst of the orange. Put all parts of the fruit in the pot.

4. Add the cinnamon sticks, nutmegs, allspice, and anise (if using).

5. Cover tightly with the lid and let simmer for at least 4 hours on low.

6. Just before serving, add the honey and brandy.

7. Pour directly into mugs and serve hot with an extra cinnamon stick (if using).

OSTARA, SPRING EQUINOX (MARCH 21 TO 23)— GENEROUSLY DEVILED EGGS

◇◇

≫ MAKES 24 DEVILED EGGS

The spring equinox is the first of the holidays on the Wheel of the Year about the total balance of light and dark. Like the autumn equinox, or Mabon, this is only one of two times during the year when hours of daylight and moonlight are equal. Ostara brings with it many blessings of balance, rebirth, and regeneration, as spring returns and life begins to grow all around.

Foods associated with fertility and abundance are commonly eaten and shared for Ostara celebrations. It is important to note that fertility foods do not just have to do with pregnancy or childbearing. Incorporate eggs into your Ostara celebrations with the intention for all your efforts in the coming season to be fertile, growing, strong, and healthy. This goes for new jobs, deeper relationships, creative projects, and financial plans. Eggs are the ultimate fertility and abundance food and can be boiled, baked, scrambled, or fried. This is not limited to chicken eggs–duck eggs and quail eggs also have the same fertility properties. As you eat and share meals made with eggs, focus on what you hope to bring into the world and what seeds you will plant this spring, willing them to grow in your vison.

YOU WILL NEED:

Large (5-quart) sauce pot
12 fresh large eggs
Large mixing bowl
Deviled egg plate or tray to hold the finished eggs
½ cup mayonnaise
2 tablespoons Dijon mustard
1 teaspoon dried dill

½ teaspoon smoked paprika
Salt
Freshly ground black pepper
Dill sprigs
Sweet baby gherkins, cut into slices resembling matchsticks (optional)

1. Fill a large sauce pot with water to a depth of about 5 inches.

2. Gently place all 12 eggs in the water, making sure they are not too crowded and have about half an inch of space between them.

3. Bring the water to a boil and continue to boil the eggs for 7 or 8 minutes on a medium gentle boil.

4. Remove from the heat and drain the water. Fill the pot back up with cold water and ice if you like to get the eggs completely cooled before peeling and cutting, or refrigerate the boiled eggs overnight before making your deviled eggs.

5. Once the eggs are cooled completely, gently peel the shells off.

6. Slice the eggs vertically down the long side of the egg, scooping the yolks into the large mixing bowl and placing the intact egg white halves on the egg tray.

7. Once all the yolks are in the bowl, mix in the mayonnaise, mustard, dill, paprika, and salt and pepper to taste. To make this mixture as creamy as possible, mash with a potato masher or mix with an electric mixer.

8. Once the yolk mixture is smooth and creamy, scoop or pipe the filling into the centers of the egg whites in 1-teaspoon portions.

9. Top with dill sprigs and baby gherkins (if using).

10. Keep chilled until ready to serve.

LITHA, SUMMER SOLSTICE (JUNE 21 TO 23)—HERB GARDEN ARUGULA PESTO

◇◇

Litha, the summer solstice, is the celebration of the longest day and the shortest night. This is the day when sunlight lasts the longest all year, and it is usually the peak of the summer growing season. It's also called midsummer by many witches and pagans because summer is the season of growing, which starts at Beltane in May and ends with the first harvest at Lammas, on August 1.

There is no shortage of festive foods around Litha. Because it is at the height of summer, it is welcomed by full beds of fresh herbs and an abundance of growing greens in gardens and grocery stores. Long days with bright sunlight into the hours of the evening make celebrating Litha the perfect time for an outdoor meal with all the flavors of the season. Adorn your solstice meal with simple foods you can eat with your hands like whole berries, melon slices, and cool sandwiches made from grilled vegetables.

This pesto is made with copious amounts of garlic and arugula for protection and prosperity magick. Using the freshest herbs possible will give this sauce a zing that really sings when topped on sandwiches, spread onto pizza crusts, brushed on chicken, or tossed with fresh tortellini. All the fresh herbs in this pesto hold prosperity energy due to the leafy green type of plants they are, especially the basil. If you want to experiment with other herbs, stick with tender leafy herbs like cilantro or dill. Herbs with a woody texture like rosemary or thyme will not blend as nicely and may overpower your pesto. For extra magickal energies, harvest any home-grown herbs from dusk to midnight on the solstice.

YOU WILL NEED:

Blender or food processor
2 tablespoons olive oil
½ cup water
Juice of 1 lemon
2 cups baby arugula
1½ cups fresh basil (leaves only)
½ cup fresh parsley
½ cup fresh mint

3 garlic cloves
1 cup Parmesan cheese
Pinch salt
Pinch freshly ground black
  pepper
¾ cup roasted pine nuts
  (optional)

1. Using a large blender or food processor, add all the pesto ingredients in the order listed above. You may have to add half and stop blending to add the rest and then continue blending depending on your appliance.

2. Blend until desired smoothness. If your pesto is too thick, add more water by the tablespoonful until it is smoother.

3. Once the pesto is smooth and looks like a thick paste, remove from the blender and store in an airtight container for up to 1 week or freeze in an airtight container for up to 3 months.

MABON, AUTUMN EQUINOX (SEPTEMBER 21 TO 23)— HARVEST BOUNTY STUFFED HEN

<><><><><><><><><><><><><><><><><><><><><><><><><><><><><><><><><>

>>> MAKES 4 STUFFED HENS

Mabon is the witch's Thanksgiving. This equinox, like Ostara, is a representation of great balance with light and dark being equal in time on this day. However, this holiday signifies the end of the growing season, or the end of the light time of the year. From this day forward, the nights become longer and the need to gather and harvest for the upcoming winter months becomes more urgent.

Because Mabon is the most richly celebrated of the three harvest festivals on the Wheel of the Year, it is often met with the largest meal of celebration. Like the contemporary American Thanksgiving holiday, a large stuffed roasted bird is not uncommon nor are pies of apple or pumpkin, cornbread stuffing, and roasted vegetables. The celebration can be large or small but always includes gratitude for the earth and its bounty.

This recipe is a twist on the secular tradition of a stuffed turkey, symbolizing a cornucopia overflowing with abundance of the harvest. It is perfect for large or intimate gatherings. Just scale this recipe accordingly. These tender hens are stuffed with a wild rice and apricot filling, then smothered in an apricot glaze, bringing in the last of the summer sun flavors mingled with the earthy flavors of autumn. A note: If there is more stuffing than can fit in the hens, serve the hens atop a pile of rice.

YOU WILL NEED:

Large skillet

1 teaspoon salt

1 teaspoon freshly ground black pepper

1 teaspoon dried rosemary

1 teaspoon dried thyme

Grated zest of 1 lemon

2 tablespoons butter

4 Cornish game hens, about 2 pounds each

1 or 2 large roasting pans

1 tablespoon olive oil

½ onion, finely chopped
2 celery stalks, finely chopped
3 garlic cloves, chopped
2 cups cooked wild rice
1 cup chopped dried apricot
1 cup sliced almonds

¼ cup chopped fresh parsley
1 jar apricot preserves
¼ cup freshly squeezed orange juice
1 tablespoon brown sugar

1. Preheat the oven to 375°F.

2. In a small bowl, combine the salt, pepper, rosemary, thyme, and lemon zest.

3. Add the butter and mix well.

4. Rub the butter mixture under and on top of the skin of each hen.

5. Put the hens in the roasting pan and set aside.

6. Make the wild rice stuffing.

7. Heat the oil in the skillet over medium heat.

8. Add the onion, celery, and garlic, cooking until just tender.

9. In a large bowl, combine the onion mixture with the cooked rice, chopped apricot, almonds, and parsley.

10. Gently scoop the rice filling into the cavity of each bird.

11. Using oven-safe kitchen twine, tie the legs of the birds together so no stuffing can fall out.

12. Cover with foil and roast the hens at 375°F for 45 to 60 minutes, or until the internal temperature reaches 175°F when tested with a meat thermometer.

13. About 10 minutes before the hens are done cooking, remove the foil and let them brown on top.

14. Just before serving, in a small pot, heat the apricot preserves, orange juice, and brown sugar until the sugar has dissolved and the consistency is pourable.

15. Spoon the apricot glaze over each hen and serve immediately.

A FINAL NOTE

Congratulations! You have made it through *Kitchen Witchcraft for Beginners*. Let this book be a springboard of inspiration and ideas as you continue to grow on your journey through food, magick, and mindfulness. With your newfound knowledge from reading this book, you will continue to deepen your connection with your own inner witch. You've learned how to set up your sacred space, how to celebrate the Wheel of the Year, and how to stock a pantry for everyday magick. You now have the mindful practices of acknowledging the work, food, energy, and intentions you feel in and around the kitchen, shining a light on the power of kitchen witchcraft.

In the kitchen or otherwise, always remember that the sacredness and magick of witchcraft comes from deep inside you. It is there now, just waiting to be expressed and brought into the world. Take what you have learned in these pages and let that magick come through your kitchen witchcraft in the form of a meal to nourish the body, mind, soul, and heart.

RESOURCES

BOOKS

Blackthorn's Botanical Brews by Amy Blackthorn. An herbalist's guide to drinks, tonics, tinctures, and teas, citing medicinal and spiritual herbalism throughout.

Cunningham's Encyclopedia of Wicca in the Kitchen by Scott Cunningham. A foundational book to use as a quick reference for energetic collocations of ingredients.

Everyday Witchcraft by Deborah Blake. A first stop for anyone looking to incorporate magick and witchcraft outside of the kitchen and into other daily practices. This is a wonderful building block to kitchen witchcraft.

Kitchen Witch: Food, Folklore & Fairy Tale by Sarah Robinson. Explores the history and lore of kitchen witches and the threads of their magick that run through today's practices.

A Kitchen Witch's Cookbook by Patricia Telesco. Beautifully describes kitchen witchcraft practices that are tangible and relatable.

The Magick of Food by Gwion Raven. Distills the nature of food magick through offerings and rituals and explains why it is so important to our spiritual and mental well-being to gather with others around food.

WitchCraft Cocktails by Julia Halina Hadas. Combines modern mixology with magickal crafts to create libations for all occasions. This book is a perfect accompaniment to magickal meal making.

PODCAST

That Witch Life podcast. Three witchy friends share their experiences as modern witches with merriment, education, and a bit of irreverence as they chat on topics from occultism to kitchen craft.

REFERENCES

"A Brief History of Sex and Chocolate." Cocoa Runners. August 24, 2021.

Brown, Dr. Amelia. "Aphrodite: Sea Goddess of the Ancient Greeks." *Neos Kosmos*. September 4, 2011. neoskosmos.com/en/2011/09/04 /dialogue/opinion/aphordite-sea-goddess-if-the-ancient-greeks.

Encyclopedia Britannica. "Cernunnos." January 12, 2021. britannica.com /topic/Cernunnos.

"The History of Avocados in America." California Avocados. June 23, 2020. californiaavocado.com/avocado101/the-history-of-california -avocados.

"The History of Chocolate." Alimentarium Historical. alimentarium.org /en/knowledge/history-chocolate.

Michelle, Heron. "Witch's 2022 Astrological Calendar for Sabbats and Esbats." Patheos.com. November 18, 2021. patheos.com/blogs /witchonfire/2021/11/witchs-2022-astrological-calendar-sabbats-esbats.

Wigington, Patti. "The Triple Goddess: Maiden, Mother and Crone, Learn Religions." January 28, 2019. learnreligions.com/maiden-mother -and-crone-2562881.

INDEX

ACKNOWLEDGMENTS

To my amazing partner and husband, Justin—thank you for brainstorms, hugs, tea, and shaking me when I am lost in self-doubt. You are forever my hero.

To my Cucina Aurora Tribe—I am ever grateful for your support, perseverance, and belief in me. Who is driving this bus anyway?

To my chosen family and all those who follow, support, encourage, and believe in my journey—thank you beyond measure.

ABOUT THE AUTHOR

 **Dawn Aurora Hunt**, owner of Cucina Aurora Kitchen Witchcraft, has been teaching and writing about kitchen witchcraft since 2010, when she started the company making gourmet foods with a dash of magick. Her previous books include *Tastes from the Temple* and *A Kitchen Witch's Guide to Recipes for Love & Romance*. She is the host of the popular Cucina Aurora Kitchen Witchcraft Podcast series, *Conversational Witchcraft*. Find out more at cucinaaurora.com or on social media @CucinaAurora.